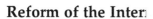
**Reform of the Inter**

**Karl Brunner Lecture Series**
Marcel Savioz, editor

John B. Taylor, *Reform of the International Monetary System: Why and How?*

# Reform of the International Monetary System:

## Why and How?

John B. Taylor

The MIT Press
Cambridge, Massachusetts
London, England

This book was set in Palatino by Westchester Publishing Services. Printed and bound in the United States of America.

Library of Congress Cataloging-in-Publication Data

Names: Taylor, John B., author.
Title: Reform of the international monetary system : why and how? / John B. Taylor.
Description: Cambridge, MA : MIT Press, [2019] | Series: Karl Brunner lecture series | Includes bibliographical references and index.
Identifiers: LCCN 2018035281 | ISBN 9780262536752 (pbk. : alk. paper)
Subjects: LCSH: International finance. | Monetary policy. | Banks and banking, International.
Classification: LCC HG3881 .T393 2019 | DDC 332.4/5--dc23 LC record available at https://lccn.loc.gov/2018035281

10   9   8   7   6   5   4   3   2

# Contents

# Series Foreword

The Swiss National Bank is grateful to John B. Taylor for writing this book in which he revisits and develops the ideas presented in his Karl Brunner Lecture on September 21, 2017. The series of books associated with the Karl Brunner Distinguished Lecture explores topics of key importance to central banking.

The Karl Brunner Distinguished Lecture Series, which is organized by the Swiss National Bank and takes place annually in Zurich, honors eminent monetary theory and policy thinkers whose research has influenced central banking. The scope of the lecture reflects the attention Karl Brunner devoted to monetary economics, his belief in the need to advance theoretical and applied analysis in this field, and in particular his concern for the policy relevance of economic science.

Thomas J. Jordan, Chairman of the Governing Board

# Preface

As with other great economists who passed away decades ago, we wonder what Karl Brunner would think and say about the unusual monetary policy around the world in the past dozen years. Of course, we can never really know. But I think we can get some excellent hints from his former student, collaborator, and friend, the great economist Allan Meltzer, who offered his views just before he died in 2017.

At a conference for central bankers and monetary experts held by the Federal Reserve Bank (Fed) of Kansas City in Jackson Hole, Wyoming, Meltzer (2016) made an important observation about monetary policy in recent years. He focused on the part of monetary policy frequently described as *quantitative easing,* a term that refers to massive increases in the size of the central bank's balance sheet, entailing large-scale purchases of financial assets. He argued that through quantitative easing, Fed policymakers had been engaging in "competitive devaluation," by which he meant a policy-induced depreciation of the exchange rate for the purposes of gaining competitive advantage for exporters and thereby stimulating the economy at the expense of other countries. He added, "Other countries have now followed and been even less circumspect about the fact that they were engaging in competitive devaluation. Competitive devaluation was tried in the 1930s, and unsuccessfully, and the result was that around that time major countries agreed they would not engage in competitive devaluation ever again." He said that he hoped that "the Federal Reserve would take the lead in trying to restore the agreement which said no more competitive devaluations," and he concluded that a reform of the international monetary system was needed.

This book is all about reforming the international monetary system. It shows *why* we need reform and explains *how* to achieve that reform. It starts by showing that there is a strong international correlation between monetary policy decisions in different countries, and concern about the exchange rate is a major cause of this correlation, much as in Allan Meltzer's explicit depiction of a world of competitive devaluation. In some cases, the exchange rate concern appears to be defensive, as central banks counteract forces from abroad that affect the exchange rate. In other cases, the exchange rate concern is offensive, as central banks endeavor to move the exchange rate to gain a competitive advantage. In all these scenarios, though, I show that the resulting international correlation of monetary policy decisions causes monetary policy to deviate from effective policies that stabilize inflation and the economy. And I show that deviations from effective monetary policy lead in turn to even greater international correlations of policy.

I then argue that rules-based reform of the international monetary system would reduce the correlation and the deviation from good policy, thereby improving economic performance. I propose a method to achieve such rules-based reform by applying basic economic theory. I then endeavor to answer deep questions about rules-based monetary policy that need to be addressed if the proposed reform is to proceed.

Finally, I show how economic theory has contributed greatly to better economic policy and performance in the past, and, if the theory is followed in practice, it can do so in the future as well.

The empirical part of the book focuses on the dozen years from 2005 to 2017, a period that includes and surrounds the Global Financial Crisis. During much of this time—especially during the latter years—many central banks actively used two separate monetary policy instruments: They used the policy interest rate, the more conventional policy instrument used in the 1980s and 1990s, but they also used the size of the balance sheet, a more unconventional policy instrument, in which reserve balances play a key role. For this reason, I develop an empirical framework for examining both the balance sheet and the interest rate instruments.

The book first considers the interest rate instrument. It draws on the existing empirical research on advanced countries and emerging-market economies, including my own research (Taylor, 2007b, 2013, 2016b), to show that in recent years, there has been an international contagion of decisions by central banks about their policy interest rates. The focus is on deviations of policy interest rates from traditional policy rules for interest rates that have worked well in the past. The contagion is due to a concern on the part of central banks about exchange rates, and in turn it has accentuated the deviations of monetary policy from standard interest rate rules that have worked well in the past.

The book then goes on to present new empirical results showing that there is a similar international contagion of decisions about the size of the balance sheet. This contagion is also due to exchange rate concerns. Here, one must distinguish—both empirically and analytically—between the central banks in large, open economies, such as the Federal

Reserve System, the European Central Bank (ECB), and the Bank of Japan (BOJ); and the central banks in smaller open economies, including those in advanced economies, such as the Swiss National Bank (SNB), and those in emerging-market economies, such as the Bank of Mexico. In large, open economies, the effects on exchange rates are harder to detect than for central banks in small, open economies.

Nevertheless, new evidence provided here reveals large and statistically significant impacts of balance sheet operations by the Fed, the BOJ, and the ECB on dollar-yen, dollar-euro, and euro-yen exchange rates. There are also large exchange rate effects of balance sheet operations in the small, open economies, where explicit foreign exchange purchases are often financed by the expansion of reserve balances. Exchange rate volatility is thus increased by monetary policy.

By considering a counterfactual policy in the estimated model, one can estimate the extent to which the policies have increased exchange rate volatility. This empirical work shows that the policy of recent years has features much like the regime of competitive devaluations described by Allan Meltzer. Moreover, after several rounds of monetary policy actions and reactions aimed at exchange rates, the international monetary system has been left with roughly the same exchange rate configuration, but much larger balance sheets to unwind.

# Acknowledgments

"Policies depend not only on theories and evidence, but on the structure of policymaking bodies and the procedures by which policies are made, implemented and changed." Thus wrote Karl Brunner and his student and lifelong coauthor, Allan Meltzer, in their introduction to *The Carnegie-Rochester Conference Series on Public Policy*, as they embarked on yet another of their many influential endeavors to connect the why and how of public policymaking. The aim of all these efforts was to "direct the attention of economists to major problems of economic policy and institutional arrangements" and to "encourage further research on policy and on the effects of national agencies and international institutions on the choice of policies."

It is in this spirit that I write this book on international monetary reform, focusing on the why—by drawing on theories and evidence—and the how—by proposing reforms of the policymaking institutions and procedures. The book is based on the annual Karl Brunner Lecture that I gave in Zurich at the Swiss Federal Institute of Technology (ETH Zurich) on September 21, 2017, and on follow-up remarks that I gave at the dinner immediately after the lecture and at a conference at the Federal Reserve Bank (Fed) of Boston a few weeks later, on October 13, 2017. The 2017 Karl Brunner Lecture, which is part of the Karl Brunner Distinguished Lecture Series established and sponsored by Swiss National Bank (SNB), was held on the tenth anniversary of the first annual SNB research conference in Zurich on September 21, 2007, at which I also gave remarks at dinner. I thank the SNB for inviting me to give the 2017 Karl Brunner Lecture and the dinner talks in both 2007 and 2017.

I first got to know Karl Brunner through his many successful endeavors to improve economics in theory and in practice, including the *Carnegie-Rochester Conference Series on Public Policy*. It was there that beginners like me had the opportunity to publish policy papers—my first being a comment on Ed Prescott's 1977 paper on time inconsistency—and to serve on the Advisory Committee (in my case, for 20 years). Other forums where he was seen putting ideas into action included the *Journal of Monetary Economics*, the *Journal of Money Credit and Banking*, and the Konstanz and Interlaken conferences. This was also the purpose of the famed Shadow Open Market Committee, which held many meetings where ideas about monetary theory informed practical recommendations about policy. Brunner started and operated many of these initiatives jointly with Allan Meltzer, who also contributed greatly to the advancement of economics in public policy.

Throughout these endeavors, I saw Karl as a brilliant, innovative economist, deeply motivated by the effective application of good economics to improve people's lives. Many public policy institutions, not only the Fed but also the International Monetary Fund (IMF), the Congressional Budget Office (CBO), and the Council of Economic Advisers, were the focus of these endeavors. A *Carnegie-Rochester* paper on the Fed by Ray Lombra and Michael Moran (1980) even investigated the Fed's institutional forecasting ability, and they found that it was actually pretty good. Karl's serious thinking, about both the ideas and the institutions of policy, was an essential (if unappreciated) contribution. Fritz Leutwiler, who served as head of the SNB and president of the Bank for International Settlements (BIS), noted that he "enjoyed very much to talk to [Brunner] and to take up some of his advice," as Allan Meltzer put it in his recent essay of appreciation of Karl (Meltzer, 2015; see also Meltzer, 1992).

Of course, Karl worked hard on his ideas, and his contributions were influential. Much of his work in monetary economics in the 1960s was summarized in his 1968 and 1971 papers (see Brunner, 1968, 1971), and most was in collaboration with Allan Meltzer, as summarized in their summa (Brunner and Meltzer, 1993), which was published after Karl's death in 1989. Their research delved into the money and credit foundations of monetary economics at a time when only a few economists—Jim Tobin, Jack Gurley, and Ed Shaw—were doing so. The Brunner-Meltzer model is, in many ways, what we economists are striving for now as we try to bring financial economics into models of monetary economics that focus on the microfoundations of credit and money.

I am particularly grateful to Thomas Jordan, chairman of the Swiss National Bank Governing Board, for his kind hospitality and generous introductions; to Cyrille Planner and the staff of the bank for their extraordinary planning and welcome; and to Emily Taber of MIT Press for excellent advice on the first draft of the book. I also wish to thank many people for their helpful comments and discussions as I prepared the talks and put the book together, including Matthew Canzoneri, V.V. Chari, John Cochrane, James Dorn, Fabian Eser, Roger Farmer, Jacob Frankel, Michele Fratianni,

Boris Hofmann, Manuel Ignacio Iribarren, Jerry Jordan, Donald Kohn, Livio Cuzzi Maya, Marcus Miller, Geovanni Olivei, David Papell, Raghu Rajan, Eric Rosengren, George Selgin, Marie-Christine Slakey, Frank Smets, and three anonymous reviewers. I would particularly like to acknowledge the staff of the Federal Reserve Bank of Boston for posing the questions through which chapter 3 is organized.

# 1    Monetary Policy Interconnections

An important empirical phenomenon, which has been documented in several research studies in recent years, is that interest rate decisions made at central banks around the world have become interrelated and highly correlated. The resulting international pattern of policy interest rates—a key monetary policy instrument of central banks—offers a revealing picture with which to begin this book. Focusing on interest rate decisions sets the stage for the more complex analysis that follows later in this book, in which we consider another instrument of monetary policy that has come to be used by central banks in recent years—the size of their balance sheets—and it enables us to explore the reasons and causes for the interrelationship between monetary policy decisions in different countries.

## 1.1   International Contagion of Deviations of Interest Rates from Policy Rules

Figure 1.1 illustrates the phenomenon nicely with two charts, through which the Bank for International Settlements (BIS), the central bank for central bankers, monitors interest rate decisions by the major central banks around the world.

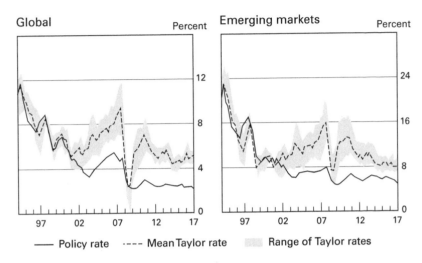

**Figure 1.1**
The Global Great Deviation. *Source*: Boris Hofmann of the BIS. The weighted average is based on 2005 GDP and purchasing power parity exchange rates. The method of calculations comes from Hofmann and Bogdanova (2012),. Here, "global" includes both advanced and emerging-market economies. The advanced economies are Australia, Canada, Denmark, the euro area, Japan, New Zealand, Norway, Sweden, Switzerland, the United Kingdom, and the United States. The emerging-market economies are Argentina, Brazil, Chile, China, Chinese Taipei, Colombia, the Czech Republic, Hong Kong SAR, Hungary, India, Indonesia, Israel, South Korea, Malaysia, Mexico, Peru, the Philippines, Poland, Singapore, South Africa, and Thailand.

The charts were originally produced by Boris Hofmann and Bilyana Bogdanova (2012), economic researchers at the BIS, to demonstrate what they dubbed the "Global Great Deviation" of interest rate decisions from commonly used policy rules, such as the Taylor rule, in which the policy interest rate reacts to inflation and real gross domestic product (GDP). The chart on the left of figure 1.1, labeled "Global," includes both advanced countries and emerging-market countries, while the chart on the right includes emerging-market countries only. The countries that the BIS puts in the advanced country group and in the emerging-market country group are listed in the note at the bottom of figure 1.1. The line labeled "Policy rate" shows the weighted average policy interest rate (usually an overnight rate or a very-short-term rate) decision for the two groups of countries. The line labeled "Mean Taylor rate"[1] shows the mean of the "range of Taylor rates" created by considering four measures of the inflation rate and the output gap that go into the policy rule. The Taylor rates are calculated based on weighted averages of the respective inflation and output gap measures for the two country groups.

Figure 1.1 shows that the interest rate decisions and the interest rates implied by the policy rule were very close to each other in the 1990s, and continued so until about 2003. But in the following years—the years leading up to the crisis in 2008—there was a large deviation: the policy rule in many central banks called for a higher policy interest rate than the actual decisions, as I pointed out for the United States in Taylor (2007c). When the crisis and the deep recession came (perhaps induced by excessive risk-taking caused by the low rates), central banks, on average, lowered their interest rates in accordance with such rules.

But starting soon after the crisis, they again began to deviate from rules-based policy, and that deviation continued throughout most of the postcrisis years. Thus, figure 1.1 reveals that central banks throughout the world—including in the emerging markets—have deviated in much the same way from this representative monetary policy rule for the interest rate.

A look at the data for each of the central banks that constitute the average of figure 1.1 shows much the same as the average. Often, there is a deviation that began before the crisis, followed by a rule-like reduction in the policy rate during the crisis, and then a period after the crisis when the rate is "too low" again. Of course, there are exceptions, such as in Brazil, where the policy rate was often above the rule; and in Australia, where the policy rate stayed close to the rule throughout the period. Nevertheless, the overall characterization of the data is clear: Both the averages and the individual country data throughout most of the world and emerging-market countries reveal correlated deviations of central bank interest rates from the policy rule for interest rates.

### 1.1.1   Central Banks Following Each Other

A simple and plausible reason for correlated deviation is that central banks tend to follow each other, resulting in a contagion of interest rate policy decisions in both the emerging-market counties and the rest of the world. Central banks follow each other, in part, because they are concerned about exchange rate appreciation: if a large foreign central bank cuts its interest rate by an unusual amount, then the home currency will tend to appreciate unless the home central bank adjusts its own interest rate down. In addition to lowering the interest rate, central banks may engage in other actions aimed at preventing an appreciation of their currency, including purchasing foreign exchange, restricting capital flows into their country, and some form of temporary macroprudential action aimed at reducing the attractiveness of international investment in their country.

These actions and reactions can occur in reverse if a large central bank increases its interest rate. Then capital tends to flow out of the other countries, deprecating their exchange rates and bringing about a central bank reaction that raises their interest rate. However, in reality, central banks might worry less about a depreciation of their exchange rate than an appreciation, which would impart a bias toward lower interest rates internationally.

Considerable econometric evidence has been reported in Taylor (2007b), Gray (2013), He and McCauley (2013), Carstens (2015), and Edwards (2017), to the effect that the deviations from domestic policy rules are directly tied to interest rate changes in other countries. This evidence is based on estimated policy rules in which one can detect the response of the interest rate in one country to changes in interest rates in another country. Such evidence is found for central banks in both advanced and emerging-market countries.

In Taylor (2007b), I included the U.S. federal funds rate in an estimated interest rate policy rule for the European Central Bank (ECB), during the period from 2001 to 2006. I found that the foreign interest rate was statistically significant; the same was true when I included a foreign interest rate in a policy rule for the United States. He and McCauley (2013) examined monetary policy in China, India, Indonesia, Malaysia, the Philippines, South Korea, Taiwan, and Thailand, and they found that "controlling for domestic inflation, output gaps and the nominal effective exchange rate, foreign interest rates have a substantial if uneven effect on domestic monetary settings in East Asia." The coefficient was as high as 0.77 in the Philippines equation and was insignificant for only one of the countries (namely, China).

Colin Gray (2013) estimated policy interest rate reaction functions using panel data from the ECB and the central banks of Australia, Canada, South Korea, the United Kingdom, Norway, New Zealand, Denmark, Israel, Brazil, China, and Indonesia. He included the U.S. federal funds rate or other measures of foreign interest rates in the equation and he found that the average reaction coefficient on the foreign interest rate was significant and large (as high as 0.75). Carstens (2015) found a significant effect of the U.S. federal funds rate in the policy rule for the Bank of Mexico, and Edwards (2017) found evidence of interest rate policy spillover in Chile and Colombia, though not in Mexico.

There is also direct evidence from those making decisions at central banks that this type of interest rate policy spillover is influenced by exchange rate concerns. I have learned this from talking with heads of central banks, who readily admit to these reactions in conversation, and from the research done by the staffs of the central banks. The Norges Bank (the central bank of Norway), for example, transparently provides a great deal of detail about interest rate decisions and the rationales for them. The policy interest rate decisions at the Norges Bank have been adjusted roughly in tandem with the interest rate decisions in the ECB in order to reduce the size of fluctuations in the exchange rate. As reviewed in Taylor (2013), the Norges Bank compares its interest rate setting to several policy rules that it used. These comparisons show that deviations of the actual policy rate below the domestic monetary policy rule (either the Taylor rule or the growth rate rule) were almost entirely due to the very low interest rate abroad. Their research also presented a policy rule with the external interest rate included; this rule comes much closer to describing the policy actions than the policy rules without external interest rates.[2]

With more than one central bank reacting to each other, this type of deviation in interest rate policy can multiply as it spreads from one country to another and moves back and forth. This multiplier can be illustrated using simple policy rules in the case of two countries shown in figure 1.2, which is based on Taylor (2013). Assume, as in the diagram in figure 1.2, that the

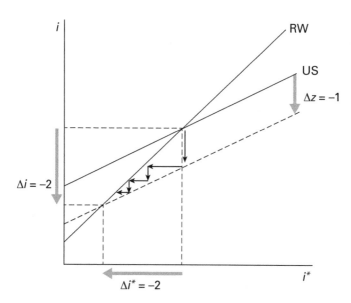

**Figure 1.2**
Illustration of the international monetary policy contagion multiplier.
*Source*: Taylor (2013).

size of the deviation from the domestic policy rule depends
on interest rate settings at the central bank in the other country.
Suppose that $i$ is the policy interest rate in one country's
central bank and $i^*$ is the policy interest rate in the other
country's central bank. Assume, for the reasons given here,
that both central banks deviate from their own policy rule by
an amount that depends on interest rate settings at the central
bank in the other country. Thus, the central banks follow
each other.

Figure 1.2 shows two reaction functions in which both
central banks react to interest rates abroad. In this example,
the first central bank has a response coefficient of 0.5 on the
second central bank's policy interest rate, and the second

central bank has a response coefficient of 1 on the first central bank's interest rate. Suppose that the first central bank cuts its interest rate $i$ by 1 percentage point below its normal policy rule setting, or by $\Delta z = -1$ in figure 1.2. Then the second central bank also will reduce its policy rate $i^*$ by 1 percentage point, which causes the first central bank to cut its interest rate by another 0.5 percentage point, leading to another cut at the second central bank, and so on. In this example, the end result is a 2-percentage-point rate cut once the iterative process settles down. The initial deviation from the policy rule of 1 percentage point by the first central bank ends up, after amplification, reducing the policy rates in both countries by 2 percentage points, or a multiplier of 2. This example also illustrates that the magnification effect requires that both countries react to developments abroad, and it provides a reason to try to limit such reactions.[3]

### 1.1.2 Alternative Explanations for the Global Great Deviation

To be sure, the pattern in figure 1.1 may be due to some common economic factors that drove interest rate decisions away from more rules-based policies at many central banks. If so, then the correlation may not reflect follow-the-leader behavior or contagion of policy, but rather a reaction to these common factors or a common assessment of other factors.

To the extent that common factors are part of the policy rule used in each country, then these factors are already accounted for in figure 1.1, and thus do not constitute an alternative explanation for the global deviation from rule-like behavior. For example, as shown in figure 1.1, the interest rate fell sharply in most countries during the commonly felt decline in real GDP and inflation at the time of the Global Financial Crisis. But that effect is already in the policy rules and the weighted average policy rule because output and inflation in each country are in the rules used by the BIS in its analysis. If anything, that common factor caused policy to be closer to rule-like behavior: The policy rule line and the policy rate line moved back in alignment during the crisis. That rule-like behavior was observed at most central banks throughout the world at that time.

Perhaps the most widely discussed common factor in the past few years has been a decline in the so-called equilibrium real interest rate, usually designated as r*. Laubach and Williams (2016) traced changes in r* going back to at least the time of the Global Financial Crisis. If a policy rule does not include a change in r* and policymakers adjust their interest rate because they observe a change in r*, then a deviation of policy from the rule will occur.

However, as the rules are calculated in figure 1.1, changes in r* are built into the policy rule at each central bank. As recorded in footnote 1, the BIS calculations include an r* term in the policy rule and allow for movements in r*. The procedure is to proxy-change r* by changes in trends of real output growth. Thus, movements in r* translate into movements in the policy rate given by the policy rule, not into deviations of the actual interest rate and the policy rate. It may be that the movements in r*, as seen by central banks, are not described well by this method. Laubach and Williams (2016) consider such changes in the trend growth rate, but they also consider shorter-term factors that shift the IS curve as well.

It is also possible that economic shocks have become more globally synchronized over time, which might lead one to list this as an alternative explanation for the global deviation shown in figure 1.1. But if those shocks are included in the policy rules of the various countries—as shocks to real GDP, inflation, and the equilibrium real interest rate are—then the increased synchronization would not lead to increased deviations from policy rules.

Yet another possibility is that there was a spread of views among central bankers around the world starting around 2003 that deviations from policy rules are appropriate. For example, the decision by the Fed to deviate in 2003–2005 from the type of policy rule that it followed in the previous two decades may have been discussed in international central bank forums and found appealing at other central banks and their research departments. I do not know of evidence for this occurring before the Global Financial Crisis, and indeed the general move then toward more rules-based inflation targeting in many emerging markets seemed to go in the opposite direction during this period.

While more research on these alternative explanations for the Global Great Deviation of interest rate decisions from more rules-based policy would be interesting and useful, my overall perspective, based on the considerations raised in this section, is that these explanations fall short in comparison with the view that central banks have followed each other in recent years concerning exchange rates and capital flows.

## 1.2   A Framework for Modeling Central Bank Balance Sheet and Interest Rate Operations

The international connections between central banks in recent years are perhaps easiest to see in the case of the interest rate instrument, but the connections also involve another instrument of policy: central bank balance sheet operations. To consider both policy instruments and thereby capture key features of the recent economic policy environment, one needs an appropriate modeling framework. The model must be different from the international model that I built in the 1980s (Taylor, 1988) to find good interest rate rules, such as the so-called Taylor (1993a) rule. In that model, there was effectively only one monetary policy instrument, which usually was the short-term interest rate. With the additional assumption in that model of capital mobility and rational expectations, it was not possible to drive exchange rates, or any other asset price, away from the fundamental paths implied by policy rules for the interest rate.

In contrast, the framework that I introduce in this book reflects the reality that central banks effectively have two disconnected policy instruments: the short-term interest rate and the supply of reserve balances on the balance sheet used to finance purchases of domestic or foreign securities. The disconnect is made possible by the payment of interest (either positive or negative) on reserve balances. Thus, if the central bank wants to expand its balance sheet without changing the interest rate, or to change its interest rate without changing its balance sheet, it uses the interest rate on reserves. In this way, a central bank can both set the interest rate and adjust the size of its balance sheet, through which it can intervene in a host of different markets. This disconnect between the two instruments enables the central bank to intervene in other markets for a variety of reasons, including allocating funds to certain sectors, dealing with the zero or effective lower bound (ELB) on interest rates, or addressing exchange rate concerns.[4]

During the years since the Global Financial Crisis and the 2007–2009 Great Recession, the central banks in larger advanced countries have purchased, on a large scale, domestic securities denominated in their own currency through their quantitative easing programs. The stated aim often has been to raise the price and reduce the yield of these domestic securities, though there are sometimes references to exchange rates. In contrast, the purchases by central banks in smaller advanced countries or emerging countries have been more explicitly aimed at exchange rates, and they accordingly have purchased foreign securities denominated in foreign currency (FC). For evidence, see, for example, Chen, Filardo, He, and Zhu (2012); Filardo and Yetman (2012); and Cukierman (2017).

To provide empirical and practical policy content to this framework in a manageable way in this book, I consider actual balance sheet data and interest rate policy in several central banks. I assume that policymakers in small, open economies can effectively take the interest rate and the balance sheets abroad as given and unaffected by their own policy. In contrast, the central banks in large countries do not take the interest rates or other actions of other central banks as given.

I consider three central banks as representing large, open economies: the Fed, the ECB, and the Bank of Japan (BOJ). I also consider the central bank in one small, open economy— the Swiss National Bank (SNB)—as representative of central banks in other small, open economies. In this way, I can consider interactions among different types of banks in a simple but revealing manner.

Given the success of this approach to investigating balance sheet policy, as described later in this chapter, a useful extension would be to include more central banks in open economies, especially emerging-market economies, in the analysis. While handling a large group of countries would be difficult econometrically, the previous section describes significant contagion effects of interest rate policy between advanced and emerging-market countries. Chen et al. (2012) show that the spillover effects of balance sheet policy are also common in emerging-market countries, including China, Hong Kong, India, South Korea, Indonesia, Malaysia, the Philippines, Singapore, Thailand, Argentina, Brazil, Chile, and Mexico.

There are, of course, both similarities and differences between the policy actions of central banks in small, open economies in recent years. Frequently, the differences are due to other country-specific factors, such as a higher historical rate of inflation. Cukierman (2017) considers key similarities and differences between the SNB and the Bank of Israel in foreign exchange operations in recent years, and more work of this kind with other central banks would be very useful.

I focus on the liability side of the balance sheet and assume that most of the purchases of assets are financed by what I will call *reserve balances*. For the Fed, purchases of dollar-denominated bonds are financed by increases in dollar-denominated reserve balances; for the BOJ, purchases of yen-denominated securities are financed by increases in yen-denominated reserve balances; for the ECB, purchases of euro-denominated securities are financed by euro-denominated reserve balances; and for the SNB, purchases of euro- and dollar-denominated securities are financed by Swiss franc–denominated reserve balances. Focusing on these assets and liabilities, the key items that change on the central bank balance sheets are shown in figure 1.3—a simplification of actual balance sheets using the approach found in Taylor (2018).

For the Federal Reserve System, reserve balances are deposits of banks at the Fed; for the BOJ, they are current account (CA) balances; for the ECB, they are current accounts plus the deposit facility (DF); and for the SNB, they are sight deposits of domestic and foreign banks and of institutions, plus other sight liabilities. Of course, there are other items on the central bank's balance sheet, including domestic currency

| Central bank in<br>large economy | | Central bank in<br>small open economy | |
| --- | --- | --- | --- |
| Assets | Liabilities | Assets | Liabilities |
| Domestic<br>securities | Reserve<br>balances | Foreign currency<br>denominated assets | Reserve<br>balances |

**Figure 1.3**
Simplified central bank balance sheet: large and small open economies

and central bank borrowing in domestic currency, but the main items used to finance quantitative easing are changes in these reserve balances. I used the term *reserve balances,* which is a common term at the Fed, while other central banks use other terms. A precise definition of reserve balances in each country is given in the appendix to this chapter.

In addition, each central bank sets its short-term policy interest rate. For the Fed, the policy rate is the federal funds rate, which is now effectively determined by setting interest on reserves because reserve balances are so high. The situation is similar in the other central banks, though the mechanisms are slightly different. The specific definitions of these policy rates are found in the Appendix to this chapter.

The private sector holds securities and deposits funds (reserve balances) at the central bank. The prices and yields are determined by market forces. The exchange rate between the euro, dollar, and Swiss franc is determined in the market, as are the prices of the bonds in each country.

The variable names and definitions considered in the modeling framework are summarized in table 1.1. The letters $R$, $I$, and $X$ represent the reserve balances, the interest rate, and the exchange rate, respectively. The subscripts $U$, $J$, $E$, and $S$ represent the central banks and their countries or

**Table 1.1**
Key Variable Names and Definitions

| | |
|---|---|
| $R_U$ | Fed, reserve balances, millions of dollars |
| $R_J$ | BOJ, CA balances, hundreds of millions of yen |
| $R_E$ | ECB, current account plus deposit facility, millions of euros |
| $R_S$ | SNB, sight deposits and other sight liabilities, millions of Swiss francs |
| $I_U$ | Effective federal funds rate, percent, dollars |
| $I_J$ | Call money rate, percent, yen |
| $I_E$ | Interest rate on deposit facility, percent, euros |
| $I_S$ | Swiss average rate overnight (Saron), percent, Swiss francs |
| $X_{JU}$ | Exchange rate, yen per one dollar |
| $X_{JE}$ | Exchange rate, yen per one euro |
| $X_{UE}$ | Exchange rate, dollars per one euro |
| $X_{SU}$ | Exchange rate, Swiss francs per one dollar |
| $X_{SE}$ | Exchange rate, Swiss francs per one euro |
| $X_{SJ}$ | Exchange rate, Swiss francs per one yen |

regions: United States, Japan, Eurozone, and Switzerland. The eight policy instruments for the four central banks, thus, are the balance sheet items (reserve balances) $R_U$, $R_J$, $R_E$, and $R_S$, and the short-term policy rates $I_U$, $I_J$, $I_E$, and $I_S$. The market-determined exchange rates are $X_{JU}$, $X_{JE}$, $X_{UE}$, $X_{SU}$, $X_{SE}$, and $X_{SJ}$.

## 1.3   The International Monetary Policy Matrix

Consider now the general empirical properties of the eight policy instruments in the four countries in recent years, focusing on the years from 2005 to 2017, which begins just before the four central banks began using the interest rate and the balance sheet in this way. This captures the major changes that occurred. I first look at the raw correlations, the time series patterns, and examples of the interactions between the interest rate and balance sheet actions. I build on the research on the relationships between the policy interest rates, as summarized in the previous section, and focus on the relationships among the balance sheets.

### 1.3.1  Patterns of Interconnections

The international monetary policy matrix shown in table 1.2 shows the correlations among all eight instruments. Several striking patterns are revealed in the matrix. First, there is a strong positive correlation between the reserve balances in each of the countries. As noted in the previous discussion of the correlation between interest rate instruments in different countries, this could indicate a direct contagion of a balance sheet action at one central bank to the balance sheet action at another central bank; or the correlation could be due to reactions to a common shock. One of the objectives of this book is to delve into these possibilities.

Second, table 1.2 reveals a strong positive correlation among the interest rate instruments in all the countries. This correlation corresponds to the recent literature on this subject reviewed in this chapter. The highest correlation in the international monetary policy matrix is between the SNB policy rate and the ECB policy rate, where the correlation coefficient is 0.93.

Third, the international monetary policy matrix shows a negative correlation between the two policy instruments in every one of the four countries: when the policy interest rate is lower, reserve balances (and thus the balance sheet) are higher. This is likely due to the common assumption at central banks that the impact of the two instruments is similar: a lower policy rate *and* an expanded balance sheet with higher reserve balances are assumed to increase aggregate demand, raise the inflation rate, and depreciate the currency.

**Table 1.2**

International Monetary Policy Matrix

Each entry shows the correlation coefficient between the policy instrument—reserve balances or the interest rate—on the row and the policy instrument on the column over the period from January 2005 to May 2017.

|        | $R_U$  | $R_J$  | $R_E$  | $R_S$  | $I_U$ | $I_J$ | $I_E$ | $I_S$ |
|--------|--------|--------|--------|--------|-------|-------|-------|-------|
| $R_U$  | 1.00   |        |        |        |       |       |       |       |
| $R_J$  | 0.72   | 1.00   |        |        |       |       |       |       |
| $R_E$  | 0.49   | 0.64   | 1.00   |        |       |       |       |       |
| $R_S$  | 0.89   | 0.85   | 0.69   | 1.00   |       |       |       |       |
| $I_U$  | −0.77  | −0.36  | −0.44  | −0.58  | 1.00  |       |       |       |
| $I_J$  | −0.53  | −0.45  | −0.37  | −0.48  | 0.49  | 1.00  |       |       |
| $I_E$  | −0.81  | −0.57  | −0.51  | −0.71  | 0.76  | 0.87  | 1.00  |       |
| $I_S$  | −0.81  | −0.62  | −0.57  | −0.72  | 0.83  | 0.81  | 0.93  | 1.00  |

Fourth, there is a uniformly negative correlation between reserve balances and the interest rates between countries. These are simple correlation coefficients, so the negative effect could be due to a negative effect in each country, coupled with a contagion effect of either the interest rate or reserve balances in each country.

## 1.3.2  Dynamic Interrelated Movements in Reserve Balances over Time

Additional information on the connection between reserve balances in different countries can be gleaned from figure 1.4, which shows the actual path of reserve balances for the Fed, the BOJ, and the ECB during a dozen years ending in 2017. The plots start in 2005, before the large increases in reserves began in 2008, to better illustrate the large magnitudes of the changes. Here, one can better see the reasons for the correlations in table 1.2 and also observe a clear temporal causality. During this period, the Fed was out in front, with large

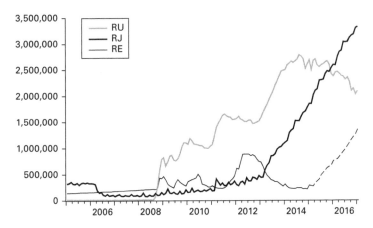

**Figure 1.4**
Reserve balances at the Fed ($R_U$), the BOJ ($R_J$), and the ECB ($R_E$), 2005–2017.
Units on the vertical axis are million dollars for $R_U$, million euros for $R_E$ and
hundred million yen for $R_J$.

increases in reserve balances, which were used to finance the
large-scale purchases of domestic securities, as the simplified
balance sheet in figure 1.3 illustrates. These purchases followed the short-lived liquidity operations during the panic
in 2008. The domestic securities consisted of mortgage-backed
securities and U.S. Treasuries. These large-scale purchases
are commonly called *quantitative easing I, II, and III*. Starting
in 2015, reserve balances began to tail off in the United States
as the securities purchases declined in size and then ended,
and currency demand grew, reducing the need for financing
the stock with reserve balances. More recently, the Fed has
reduced the size of its portfolio of domestic securities, lessen-
ing the need for financing via reserve balances.

As figure 1.4 shows, this expansion of reserve balances in
the United States was followed by a similar move by the BOJ
at the start of 2013. After Shinzō Abe was elected prime min-

ister of Japan, he chose Haruhiko Kuroda to be the governor of the BOJ. Kuroda began to buy domestic securities financed by reserve balances. That increase had yet to diminish by 2017, though there was occasional talk and consideration of a tapering. Then, starting in late 2014 after a well-publicized speech by Mario Draghi, the president of the ECB, in August at Jackson Hole, Wyoming, that bank started increasing reserve balances in earnest. (The dashed lines in figure 1.4 for reserve balances at the ECB in later periods are due to less than quarterly reporting, as I will discuss later in this chapter.)

There is a real sense, therefore, that these three central banks have followed each other with these policies during this period. The increase in reserve balances first began in the United States, was followed in Japan, and then continued in the Eurozone. In the end, the increase in global liquidity was much larger than if there had not been this contagion. An important question is whether the central banks were simply trying to provide liquidity or whether the actions are part of a competitive devaluation process.

For the interest rate instrument, as described previously, a common research method is to measure the reaction of central banks to other countries' interest rate decisions by including the foreign central bank's interest rate in the reaction function. This is much more difficult in cases where the balance sheet is the instrument because there is no comparable estimated or theoretical reaction function to employ; however, Piotr Skolimowski (2017) reports that Louis Harreau of Credit Agricole is endeavoring to do so. Moreover, there appears to be a delay of uncertain length between the action of one central bank and the reaction of the other.

Nevertheless, it may be of interest to report the effects of including other central bank reserve balances in a reaction function for each country's reserve balances. If there were no other forcing variables in the equation—such as the inflation rate or real GDP—we can think of the error term in the equation as driving each country's reserve balances. Consider, for example, a reaction function in which reserve balances in Japan move contemporaneously in response to reserve balances in the United States, and reserve balances in the United States in turn respond contemporaneously to reserve balances in Japan. Simple estimated regression equations along these lines are presented here for the sample period from January 2005 to May 2017, with t-statistics in parentheses:

$$R_J = -108 + 0.76R_U + e$$

$$(-1.2) \quad (13.4)$$

$$R_U = 647 + 0.72R_J + v$$

$$(9.01) \quad (13.37)$$

As with the interest rate reactions illustrated in the two-dimensional diagram in figure 1.2, one could calculate an international multiplier effect for reserve balances from these two equations. The ultimate reaction to a shock ($v$) in the United States would be to increase reserve balances by about twice as much as called for in the original policy rule equation after the series of back-and-forth reactions take place. This is comparable to the interest rate reaction functions illustrated in figure 1.2. A 1-unit move in $v$ is associated with an increase in $R_U$ by $(1 - 0.76 \times .072)^{-1} = 2.2$. However, without a formal rationale for such responses, we cannot assume that these coefficients are stable or that the effects do not occur with a lag. In the next section, we consider a more formal explanation of such reactions, which involve the effect on exchange rates.

## 1.4 Impact of the Balance Sheet on Exchange Rates: Yen, Euro, Dollar

To determine whether the exchange rate may be a factor in the central bank balance sheet decisions, we need to examine the impact of these decisions on exchange rates. For this purpose, I consider the following model:

$$X_{JU} = \alpha_0 + \alpha_1 R_J + \alpha_2 R_U + \alpha_3 R_E$$

$$X_{JE} = \beta_0 + \beta_1 R_J + \beta_2 R_U + \beta_3 R_E$$

$$X_{UE} = \gamma_0 + \gamma_1 R_J + \gamma_2 R_U + \gamma_3 R_E,$$

in which the exchange rates between the U.S. dollar, the yen, and the euro depend on reserve balances at each central bank. These equations are like inverted money demand equations, where *money* is the amount of reserve balances, or deposits, held by banks at the central bank. There is no need for a scale variable, such as income or GDP, as in a classic money demand model, because the movements in reserves are quite large relative to scale variables during this period. While one could put reserve balances on the left side of the equations rather than on the right side, the exchange rate variables, which would then be on the right, have more short-term volatility, and their impacts thus are more difficult to estimate.

The economic rationale for the equations is as follows: If banks are to be willing to hold more yen-denominated reserves $R_J$, they must expect the yen to appreciate relative to the dollar and the euro; thus, $\alpha_1$ and $\beta_1$ should be positive because the depreciation of the yen or euro makes their subsequent appreciation more likely. The same reasoning suggests that $\alpha_2 < 0$ and $\gamma_2 > 0$, and that $\beta_3 < 0$ and $\gamma_3 < 0$. During much of this time, especially during the postcrisis period, the interest rate varied very little, essentially hovering around zero, so changes in expected return likely were dominated by these exchange rate movements.

### 1.4.1   Regression Results

The least squares regression results are shown in table 1.3. As with the correlation matrix and the charts, the sample period begins in 2005 and goes into 2017 with slight differences in the starting and ending months in each equation.

When interpreting the size of the regression coefficients in table 1.3, recall that reserve balances are measured in millions for the Fed ($2,225,769), the ECB (1,631,073 euros), and the SNB (552,694.9 Swiss francs), and in hundreds of millions for the BOJ (3,516,854 yen)—the levels of reserve balances are shown in parentheses for May 2017. Recall also that the exchange rates are in U.S. dollars per euro (1.105), Japanese yen per euro (124.03), and Japanese yen per U.S. dollar (112.24). Thus, the coefficients are quite small, and they are smallest for the dollar per euro regressions.

In all respects, the theoretical predictions are confirmed by the data:

**Table 1.3**
Impact of Balance Sheet Changes on Exchange Rates

The sample for the $X_{JU}$ regression equation is from May 2005 to May 2017. The samples for the $X_{JE}$ and $X_{UE}$ regression equations are from January 2005 to January 2017. Here, t-values are shown in parentheses.

|  | Constant | $R_J$ | $R_U$ | $R_E$ | $R^2$ |
|---|---|---|---|---|---|
| $X_{JU}$ (¥/$) | 113.0 (97.4) | 2.10E-05 (19) | −1.22E-05 (−13) | −3.17E-05 (−12) | 0.74 |
| $X_{JE}$ (¥/€) | 153.6 (83.7) | 1.56E-05 (8.8) | −1.20E-05 (8.2) | −4.88E-05 (−11) | 0.61 |
| $X_{UE}$ ($/€) | 1.366 (105) | −1.06E-07 (−8.5) | 3.85E-08 (3.7) | −7.45E-08 (−2.3) | 0.51 |

- An increase in reserve balances $R_J$ at the BOJ causes $X_{JU}$ and $X_{JE}$ to rise;, in other words, it causes the yen to depreciate against the dollar and the euro.
- An increase in reserve balances $R_U$ at the Fed causes $X_{JU}$ to fall and $X_{UE}$ to rise; in other words, it causes the dollar to depreciate against the yen and the euro.
- An increase in reserve balances $R_E$ at the ECB causes $X_{JE}$ and $X_{UE}$ to fall; in other words, it causes the euro to depreciate against the yen and the dollar.

For completeness, I have included the cross-effects, such as the impact on the dollar-per-euro rate when $R_J$ at the BOJ increases. In this case, this action causes the euro to depreciate against the dollar.

The estimated effects are large and highly significant. The regressions demonstrate strong balance sheet (quantitative easing) effects on exchange rates in all three countries. While several economists and market analysts—including Allan Meltzer, quoted in the Preface of this book—discussed these effects, to my knowledge, this is the first study to demonstrate the impact statistically.

The results are also consistent with policy narratives of how and why decisions were made during this period. During the period of quantitative easing and expansion of reserve balances in the United States, the yen significantly appreciated against the dollar, and this continued as the Fed extended its large-scale asset purchase program, financed with increases in reserve balances with little or no response from the BOJ. Recall that the currency appreciation in Japan became a key issue in the 2012 election, and when Shinzō Abe was elected prime minister, he appointed Haruhiko Kuroda, under whom the BOJ implemented its own quantitative easing. Associated with this change in policy was a depreciation of the yen. The subsequent moves of the ECB toward quantitative easing were similarly due to concerns about an appreciating euro. At the Jackson Hole conference in August 2014, ECB president Mario Draghi spoke about these concerns and suggested quantitative easing. This subsequent shift in policy was followed by a weaker euro. Evidence of these impacts is found in the estimated equations.

To be sure, there is a good deal of serial correlation in the error terms in these equations, which may bias the estimates of the standard errors of the coefficients. For this reason, I also estimated the standard errors with the Newey-West (1987) correction. This does not affect the point estimates, but it does raise the estimated standard errors of the coefficients and lower the estimated t-statistics. In the yen-per-dollar equation, the t-values become 50.2, 10.0, −6.9, and 8.6, respectively; in the yen-per-euro equation, the t-values become 35.0, 5.1, −3.9, and −9.5, and in the euro-per-dollar equation, the t-values become 40. 8, −5.6, 1.8, and −1.6.

### 1.4.2   Impact on Exchange Rate Stability

One way to measure the impact of the balance sheet operations on exchange rate volatility is to compare the volatility of the exchange rate under the counterfactual of no changes in reserve balances with the actual volatility, using the equations in table 1.3. For the yen-per-dollar equation, the standard error of the regression is 7.27 and the standard deviation of the dependent variable is 14.11, indicating that the movements in reserve balances have nearly doubled the volatility of the exchange rate. For the yen-per-euro equation, the standard error of the regression is 11.3 and the standard deviation of the dependent variable is 18.03, indicating that the movements in reserve balances have increased the volatility of the exchange rate by 60 percent. For the euro-per-dollar equation, the standard error of the regression is 0.080 and the standard deviation of the dependent variable is 0.112, indicating that the movements in reserve balances have increased the volatility of the exchange rate by 40 percent.

### 1.4.3 Charts Behind the Scenes

The statistical findings reported in table 1.3 can be further understood using the three panels in figure 1.5. In the top portion of each panel, I show the same time series patterns of reserve balances; in the lower portion of each panel, I show a different pair of exchange rates. In the first panel, one can see the dollar getting weaker against the yen until the BOJ acts, and the dollar then strengthens against the yen. In the second and third panels, one can see the weakening of the euro against the dollar and the yen after the action by the ECB.

### 1.4.4 Narrowing in on the Euro-Dollar Exchange Rate and ECB Balance Sheet Operations

The exchange rate effect is more noticeable in figure 1.6, which simply shows the euro-to-dollar exchange rate and the increase in reserve balances by the ECB.

One can better visualize the impacts by looking at the fitted and actual values of the estimated exchange rate equation, in which the euro-to-dollar exchange rate is regressed only on the reserve balances $R_E$ in the ECB. The estimated equation is $X_{EU} = 1.41 - 2.36\text{E-}07 * R_E$, where the t-values are 82.2 and −8.1, respectively, and $R^2 = 0.42$. The fitted and actual values are shown in figure 1.7. Note the close relation between the fitted and actual values throughout the period. The large depreciation of the euro and the increase in $R_E$ are seen near the end of the sample. The depreciation begins in advance of the actual move in reserve balances because the move had been signaled clearly in advance.

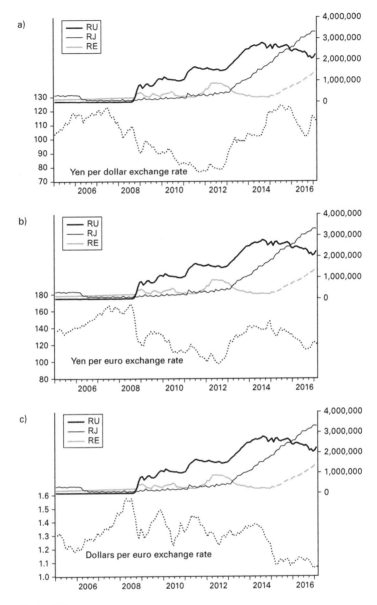

**Figure 1.5**
Exchange rates and reserve balances, 2005–2017

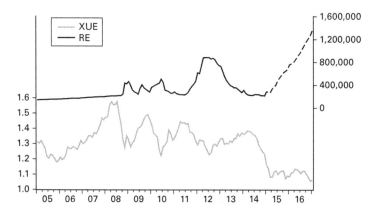

**Figure 1.6**
The euro-to-dollar exchange rate and reserve balances at the ECB

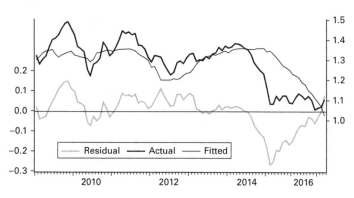

**Figure 1.7**
Actual and fitted values from simple regression of $X_{EU}$ on $R_E$

### 1.4.5 Missing Observations at the ECB and Robustness Checks with Weekly Data

Note that the monthly reserve balance series ($R_E$) in figures 1.5 and 1.6 exhibits gaps. These are due to missing observations in the current account and deposit facility, as downloaded from the ECB website. The reason for the missing observations is that there are no data collected for the months in which a new reserve maintenance period was not started. Before 2014, the ECB met and decided on monetary policy once a month, so a new reserve maintenance period started every month. But starting in the beginning of January 2015, the ECB decreased the frequency of its meetings and monetary policy decisions to about every six weeks. As a result, there are months in which no new maintenance period starts, and where the monthly data sets include no value for current accounts and deposit facilities (thus the missing observations for $R_E$).

If one were interested only in the minimum reserve requirement, it would be appropriate for those months with gaps to take the previous month's value because the reserve requirement does not change in between. However, for the current account and deposit facility, using this approach for the monthly series makes less sense because these series change, even in months where there is no monetary policy meeting. The ECB is currently looking for a statistical procedure to create a more meaningful monthly series. In the meantime, it is possible to check for robustness in these results by using weekly rather than monthly observations for current accounts and deposit facilities, and thus $R_E$.

Figure 1.8 shows the weekly data series, which can be compared with the monthly data in figure 1.6. The patterns are quite similar and can be checked with the regression equations, which are also quite similar.

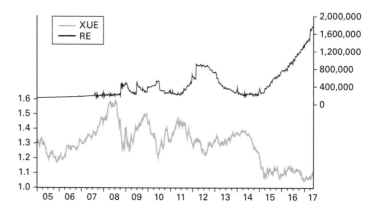

**Figure 1.8**
Weekly observations: euro-dollar exchange rate and reserve balances at ECB

If one uses weekly data and regresses the euro-to-dollar exchange rate on the reserve balances $R_E$ in the ECB, one obtains the following estimated equation: $X_{EU} = 1.38 - 2.09E-07^*R_E$, where the t-values are 214.5 and −17.7, respectively, and $R^2 = 0.33$.

## 1.5 Balance Sheet and Exchange Rate Interactions in Small, Open Economies

Now let us consider how small, open economies react to these international developments focusing on actions at the SNB related to movements of the Swiss franc. The graph in figure 1.9 shows the recent history of the Swiss franc against the euro and the dollar. The graph shows that the period since the Global Financial Crisis can be divided into three phases. During this period, the large central banks were all expanding their balance sheets, as discussed in the previous section, and the SNB was as well.

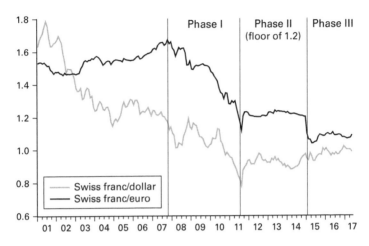

**Figure 1.9**
The Swiss franc against the dollar and the euro

During the first phase, the Swiss franc appreciated even though the SNB intervened to try to prevent that from happening by buying dollars and euros. In the second phase, which began in September 2011, the SNB indicated that it would intervene in unlimited amounts to prevent the franc from moving below a floor of 1.2 francs per euro. The stated reason was that the strong currency posed a threat to the economy and could cause deflation. As Clarida (2016) argues, "this was a response that they likely never would have considered had there not been a crisis next door." The third phase began in January 2015, around the time of the ECB's move toward quantitative easing and the large increases in reserve balances at the ECB shown in figure 1.2.

### 1.5.1  Balance Sheet Expansion and Foreign Currency (FC) Purchases

The foreign exchange purchases were mostly euro-denominated and dollar-denominated. In 2016, of the 696 billion purchases in terms of Swiss francs, 321 billion were in euros and 309 billion were in dollars. Most of the purchases were financed by sight deposits of banks and sight liabilities. As described earlier, I call the sum of these amounts *reserve balances,* and I label them $R_S$ in the chart. Figure 1.10 shows that the SNB has increased its holdings of FC investments (i.e., in euros and dollars) substantially since the crisis, and $R_S$ tracks these FC holdings very closely. The timing appears to be closely related to its efforts to prevent appreciation of the Swiss franc due to movements emanating from the ECB and the Fed.

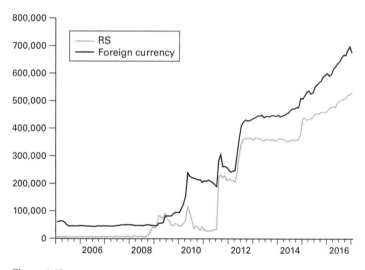

**Figure 1.10**
Reserve balances and foreign currency purchases by the SNB

Millions of CHF

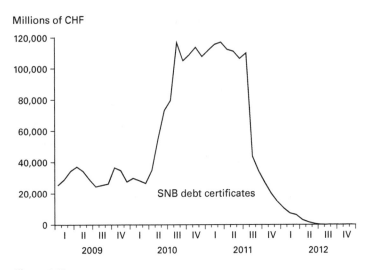

SNB debt certificates

**Figure 1.11**
SNB debt temporarily increased in 2010 and 2011

To be sure, some of the purchases were financed by other means, including by issuing currency and issuing SNB debt. For example, figure 1.11 shows that in 2010 and 2011, some of the initial purchases of foreign exchange were financed by the issuance of SNB debt certificates. One can see the gap between reserve balances ($R_S$) and FC purchases in figure 1.10, which corresponds to the temporary increase in debt certificates in figure 1.11. Nevertheless, most of the increase in FC purchases was financed by reserve balances.

Figure 1.12 shows the close relation between the franc-euro exchange rate ($X_{SE}$) and reserve balances ($R_S$) at the SNB during this period. It also shows the reaction of $R_S$ to the movements of the exchange rate. Here, the SNB increased its reserve balances and bought euros and dollars to try to limit the appreciation of the Swiss franc. While figures 1.10 and

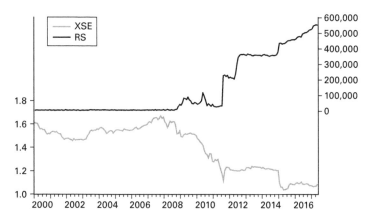

**Figure 1.12**
Reserve balances ($R_S$) and the Swiss franc-euro exchange rate ($X_{SE}$)

1.12 together provide convincing evidence that the balance sheet expanded in response to exchange rate pressure, they do not show the impact of the purchases on the exchange rate, which would go in the opposite direction.

### 1.5.2   Two-Way Causality between $R_S$ and $X_{SE}$

To see the impact of the policy on the exchange rate, as well as the reaction function of policy, we can examine the impulse response functions from a vector autoregression (VAR) of the Swiss franc exchange rate and the expansion of the balance sheet. We use the level of $R_S$ rather than the change, under the assumption that the demand for reserves is in levels. An estimated VAR is shown in table 4. It is estimated over the period that includes the Global Financial Crisis.

Granger causality tests show that there is a strong two-way causality: The hypothesis that $R_S$ does not Granger-cause $X_{SE}$ is rejected with an F-statistic of 4.74; and the hypothesis that $X_{SE}$ does not Granger-cause $R_S$ is rejected with an F-statistic

**Table 1.4**
VAR: $X_{SE}$ and SNB Reserves ($R_S$)
Sample: May 2000—May 2017, t-values in parentheses

|              | $X_{SE}$    | $R_S$      |
| ------------ | ----------- | ---------- |
| $X_{SE}$ (−1) | 1.24        | −72096.0   |
|              | (6.9)       | (−1.1)     |
| $X_{SE}$ (−2) | −0.305      | −9489.1    |
|              | (−2.6)      | (−0.089)   |
| $X_{SE}$ (−3) | 0.17        | −60825.5   |
|              | (1.5)       | (−0.58)    |
| $X_{SE}$ (−4) | −0.099      | 95919.1    |
|              | (−1.4)      | (1.4)      |
| $R_S$ (−1)   | 3.47E-07    | 1.02       |
|              | (4.3)       | (13.8)     |
| $R_S$ (−2)   | −3.76E-07   | −0.107     |
|              | (−3.09)     | (−0.95)    |
| $R_S$ (−3)   | 6.50E-08    | 0.031      |
|              | (0.52)      | (0.27)     |
| $R_S$ (−4)   | −2.68E-08   | 0.019      |
|              | (−0.33)     | (0.25)     |
| Constant     | −0.0189     | 72404.2    |
|              | (−0.7)      | (2.9)      |
| $R^2$        | 0.99        | 0.99       |

of 4.04. In other words, changes in the exchange rate Granger-cause an expansion of $R_S$; and in turn, the expansion of $R_S$ Granger-causes changes in the exchange rate.

The impulse response functions can be computed from this VAR. These are shown in figure 1.13, along with 95 percent confidence bands, which indicate a strong statistical significance. The lower-left panel shows that the SNB reacts to an appreciating Swiss franc ($X_{SE}$ down) by increasing $R_S$ (buying euros and dollars financed by $R_S$). The upper-right

Response to One Standard Deviation with SE Bands

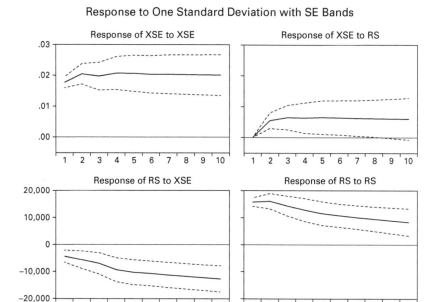

**Figure 1.13**
Impulse response function: $R_S$ and $X_{SE}$

panel shows that the Swiss franc depreciates (i.e., $X_{SE}$ goes up) when the SNB increases $R_S$ (i.e., buys foreign exchange).

While the data in this empirical exercise are drawn from the experience in Switzerland and the SNB, the mechanism is common to other small, open economies. I have found that a similar pattern of causality exists when the policy instrument is the interest rate rather than the balance sheet: The differential between the SNB policy rate and the ECB policy rate affects the degree to which the Swiss franc is attractive compared with the euro. The impulse response function shows that a depreciation of the Swiss franc leads to a rise in the Swiss interest rate relative to the euro rate, and a rise in the interest rate causes the Swiss franc to appreciate relative to the euro.

### 1.5.3   Balance Sheet Contagion Again

Now, let us examine the dynamic relationship between $R_S$ and $R_E$ or $R_U$. Recall that the correlation matrix in table 1.2 shows a very close correlation between $R_S$ and both $R_U$ and $R_E$. This is clear in the graph in figure 1.14, below which is shown the time-series patterns between the sum $R_U + R_E$ and $R_S$. This balance sheet contagion between the SNB and the Fed or the ECB is thus very similar to the balance sheet contagion observed between the Fed and the ECB.

The economic underpinning of this connection is clear. The expansion of reserve balances at the Fed or the ECB has impacts on the exchange rate, tending to depreciate the currency and appreciate the Swiss franc. The reaction function of

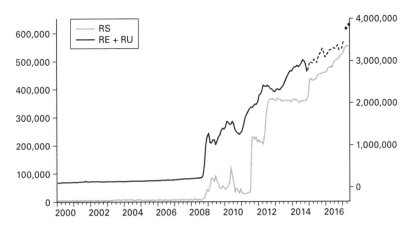

**Figure 1.14**
Reserve balances: $R_S$ and $R_E + R_U$

the SNB to a stronger currency is to intervene in the exchange markets by buying either dollars or euros. Because these are largely financed by reserve balances, the ultimate effect is for reserve balances to follow each other. Although the actions by the Fed and the ECB are not necessarily aimed at the Swiss franc, they put upward pressure on that currency, which elicits a response by the SNB.

## 1.6 Policy Implications for the International Monetary System

I have shown thus far in this chapter that there are significant international connections between central bank interest rate decisions and balance sheet decisions in different countries. For both policy instruments, the exchange rate is a factor causing deviations from policy strategies that have worked well in the past.

I also showed that there are significant exchange rate effects of balance sheet operations, both for the large, advanced countries that are not explicitly intervening in exchange markets and for small, open economies that have little choice but to react to prevent unwanted moves in their own exchange rates. This exchange rate effect is likely to be a factor behind balance sheet actions taken by some central banks and the reason for the contagion in recent years as countries endeavor to counteract other countries' actions to influence exchange rates. In this sense, there is a "competitive devaluation" aspect to these actions, as argued by Allan Meltzer (2016, p. 493), whether they are intentional or not.

The resulting movements in exchange rates are a source of instability in the global economy, as they affect the flow of goods and capital and interfere with their efficient allocation. They also are a source of political instability, as concerns about currency manipulation are heard from many sides. Moreover, as countries have used balance sheet operations to neutralize the impact on their own currencies, balance sheets have grown and multiplied throughout the world, and this has raised concerns about the impact of drawing down these balance sheets. As the Secretary of the U.S. Treasury Henry Morgenthau (1944, p. 2) said long ago, there are many reasons to "do away with economic evils—competitive currency devaluations and destructive impediments to trade."

It is difficult to determine for sure whether exchange rates have been more volatile because of these monetary policies. However, a counterfactual exercise using the estimated model presented in this chapter shows that exchange rates would have been significantly less volatile if balance sheet operations had not been used in this way in recent years.

There is also the corroborating evidence that exchange rate volatility and capital flow volatility have increased in recent years as monetary policy has changed. For example, the standard deviation of the 12-month percent change in the U.S. dollar index against major currencies as defined by the Fed has increased: For the period from the end of the Plaza Accord in January 1988 through June 2002, the approximate date at which there was a shift away from rules-based policy as discussed in Taylor (2016b), the standard deviation of the percent change in this index was 5.7 percent. It then increased to 8.3 percent from June 2002 to September 2017. The range also increased, from −12 to 12 to −15 to 20.

According to Rey (2013), Carstens (2015), Coeuré (2017), and Ghosh, Ostry, and Qureshi (2017), exchange rate volatility, capital flow volatility, or both have increased recently. Rey (2013) found that a global financial cycle, which was driven in part by monetary policy, affected credit flows in the international financial system. Carstens (2015) documented a marked increase in the volatility of capital flows to emerging markets in recent years. To be sure, there are other explanations for this volatility, suggesting the need for more research. Ghosh et al. (2017) argue that the volatility has increased because of international externalities and market imperfections. Nevertheless, the evidence provided here and in other recent studies suggests that monetary policy has been part of the problem.

### 1.6.1   A Rules-Based International Monetary System without Competitive Devaluations

The main policy implication of this analysis is that there should be a reform that makes the institutional procedures of policymaking more conducive to a rules-based international monetary system without the threat of competitive devaluation. The international economy, thereby, would be more stable with a more rules-based international monetary system.

But how could such a system be implemented? Should there be an international agreement? Should the Fed "take the lead in trying to restore the agreement which said no more competitive devaluations," as Allan Meltzer (2016, p. 494) put it? An agreement of this sort was embedded in the Articles of Agreement of the International Monetary Fund (IMF) when they were adopted by the United States in 1944.

A practical approach would be for each central bank to describe and commit to a monetary policy rule or strategy for setting the policy instruments (Taylor, 2015, 2016b). The rules-based commitments would remove some of the reasons why central banks have followed each other in recent years. Because each central bank would know what other central banks are doing, the banks will not need to guess one another's behavior and try to make ad hoc adjustments. For example, if the Fed lowers its interest rate for reasons that are clearly part of a strategy, other central banks can properly adjust their interest rate according to their own strategies without deviating from them. By transparently reporting their monetary policy strategies, central banks would automatically create a global system that works well, at least according to economic history and economic models.

The strategy in each country could include a specific inflation target, a list of key variables to react to in certain specified ways, and an estimate of the equilibrium interest rate using, for example, the method employed by the BIS in figure 1.1. The process would not impinge on other countries' monetary strategies. It would be a flexible exchange rate system, though currency zones like the Eurozone, and the central banks could certainly be part of it.

Such a system would pose no threat to either the national or international independence of central banks. Each central bank would formulate and describe its strategy. Central banks participating in the process would not have a say in the strategies of other central banks, other than that the strategies be reported. And the strategies could be changed or deviated from if the world changed or if there were an emergency. An agreed-on procedure for describing the change and the reasons for it would be useful. It is possible that some central banks will include foreign interest rates in the list of variables they react to, as suggested by Carstens (2016), so long as it is transparently described. But when they see other central banks not doing so, they will likely do less of it, recognizing the amplification effects. The agreement would be completely global rather than for a small group of countries. As with the process that led to the Bretton Woods system, it could begin informally with a small group and then spread out.

Many have called for reforms of the international monetary system, reflecting concerns about instability, international policy spillovers, volatile capital flows, and poor economic performance. So, the time might be right for reform. The BIS has been researching the issues, and Jaime Caruana, the former general manager of the BIS, has promoted reform. Paul Volcker (2014) argued that "the absence of an official, rules-based, cooperatively managed monetary system has not been a great success." Raghu Rajan (2016, p. 3) added that "what we need are monetary rules that prevent a central bank's domestic mandate from trumping a country's international responsibility." Mario Draghi (2016) argued, "We would all clearly benefit from … improving communication over our reaction functions."

The international rules-based approach is attractive because each country can choose its own independent strategy and simultaneously contribute to global stability. These advantages of an international rules-based system based on monetary policy rules in each country were stressed by Karl Brunner and Allan Meltzer (1993, p. 232) in their comprehensive *summa*. They wrote, "An international rule for compatible monetary policies creates a public good … There would be no international agreement and no reason to impose the costs of a coordinating organization. Each country would choose its own course."

The major central banks now have explicit inflation goals, and many policymakers use policy rules that describe strategies for the policy instruments. Thus, explicit statements about policy goals and strategies to achieve these goals are feasible. Having a wide agreement that some form of international reform is needed would help move the implementation along. In any case, a clear commitment by the Fed to move in this rules-based direction would help. So too would

legislation in the United States to require that the Fed report
its rules-based strategy, such as that which has been working
its way through the U.S. Congress.

The biggest hurdle to an agreement is a disparity of views
about the problem and the solution. Some are not convinced
of the importance of rules-based monetary policy; others
may doubt that it would deal with the problems of volatile
exchange rates and capital flows. Some believe that the competitive depreciations of recent years are simply part of a
necessary process of world monetary policy easing.

### 1.6.2 The Nash Equilibrium Is Nearly an Internationally Cooperative Equilibrium

Earlier research, such as in Taylor (1985), helps address such
concerns. The findings from such research show that there
would be little additional gain from the central banks jointly
optimizing their policies. In other words, the *Nash equilibrium*, in which each country chose its monetary strategy
while taking as given other countries' strategies, is nearly
optimal, or nearly an internationally cooperative equilibrium. Moreover, in practice, attempts to deviate from existing
strategies could lead to unintended suboptimal behavior,
as when Japan raised its interest rate to help lower the
value of the dollar as agreed to in the 1985–86 Plaza Accord
between Japan, Germany, France, the United Kingdom, and
the United States.

In the models used in this research, real exchange rate
affects output, capital is mobile, rigidities exist (including
that prices and wages are sticky), and cross-country linkages
connect the prices of foreign imports to domestic prices.
Central bankers face a macroeconomic trade-off between
price stability and output stability, and they have the task of
finding a policy strategy in which they adjust their monetary

policy instrument to reach an optimal point on that trade-off. The strategy must respond to shocks while not creating its own shocks, either domestically or internationally

The trade-off is like a frontier. Monetary policy cannot take the economy to infeasible positions off the frontier. But suboptimal monetary policy—reacting to policy deviations, the wrong variables, etc.—can take the economy to inferior points from the trade-off. Along the frontier, lower price variability can be achieved only with greater output variability corresponding to different values of the reaction coefficients. The existence of such a trade-off is quite general, and the modeling framework has been used in many monetary policy studies going back to the 1970s and continuing today.

The multicountry models imply that a central bank's choice of a policy strategy has little impact on the outputs and price stability trade-offs in the other countries. Thus, there is little to be gained by countries coordinating their choice of policy rules with other countries if all of them are following policy rules that are optimal domestically. The converse situation, in which monetary policy in one or more countries deviates from the policy rule, is less clear cut theoretically because it requires defining the nature of the deviation.

Nevertheless, the trade-off concept can be used to illustrate how such deviations from an optimal policy rule can lead to a breakdown in the international system: Suppose that a country deviates from its policy rule and moves in the direction of an inefficient policy. There are two types of impacts on other countries. First, the trade-off in other countries shifts in an unfavorable direction, perhaps due to more volatile capital flows, exchange rates, commodity prices, and export demand. Second, less efficient monetary policy in one country brings about a less efficient monetary policy in other countries as well. For example, if a policy change in one country brings about an excessively easy policy with very low interest rates, then the policymakers in other countries—concerned about exchange rate appreciation—may deviate from their policy rule by setting interest rates that are too low.

### 1.6.3   Global Normalization

A prerequisite for this reform would be for the global international monetary system to normalize. Getting back to a balance sheet with a level of reserves close to the normal level observed before the crisis will require that the Fed and other large central banks gradually reduce their securities holdings. If they wait the long time required in order for currency growth to create the normalization, the transition period will be so long that the present level of reserve balances will seem permanent.

It is also essential that the normalization be predictable and strategic, so as not to cause market turbulence (Taylor, 2008). That lesson was learned from the so-called "taper tantrum" in May 2013, when Fed chair Ben Bernanke indicated in a hearing before the Joint Economic Committee of the U.S. Congress that in "the next few meetings," the size of the purchases of securities might diminish, and market turbulence increased for a while as a result. As soon as the tapering strategy was announced in advance and thus became more predictable, the markets digested it very easily.

The Fed's statement in its September 2014 (p. 1) "Policy Normalization Principles and Plans," to the effect that the Federal Open Market Committee (FOMC) "intends to reduce the Federal Reserve's securities holdings in a gradual and predictable manner," is consistent with this approach. And the "Addendum to the Policy Normalization Principles and Plans," issued in 2017, continued with more details. The FOMC said that it intends to reduce the Fed's securities holdings gradually by decreasing its reinvestment of principal payments to the extent that they exceed gradually rising levels.

### 1.6.4   Reestablishing a Connection between the Interest Rate and Reserve Balances

A companion proposal about the eventual size of reserve balances and the balance sheet would also be helpful. Yes, normalization of the balance sheet in a predictable, strategic way is important, but so is providing a sense of what normal is. In my view, after the normalization period, or after this transition is finished, the policy interest rate should again be determined by market forces. In other words, it would be useful to reestablish the connection between interest rate policy and balance sheet policy, as defined in this book.

While one might argue that the pace of reduction of the balance sheet could be faster, it is important that the statement now says that the supply of reserve balances will decline by set amounts; this reduces uncertainty and lowers the chances of market disruption. But there is still a great deal of uncertainty about the eventual size of the balance sheet that the Fed and other central banks are aiming for. As stated in the FOMC's 2017 Addendum (p. 1), the "Committee currently anticipates reducing the quantity of reserve balances, over time, to a level appreciably below that seen in recent years but larger than before the Global Financial Crisis; the level will reflect the banking system's demand for reserve balances and the Committee's decisions about how to implement monetary policy most efficiently and effectively in the future. The Committee expects to learn more about the underlying demand for reserves during the process of balance sheet normalization."

Central banks could be more specific about the eventual size and configuration of the balance sheet, as the range of uncertainty remains very large. They could say that they are aiming for an eventual balance sheet and a corresponding level of reserve balances in which the interest rate is determined by the demand and supply of reserves—in other words, by market forces—rather than by an administered rate on reserve balances. Conceptually, this means that the Fed and many other central banks would be operating under a framework as they did in the decades before the crisis; according to those with experience at the open market trading desk at the New York Fed at that time, such as Peter Fisher who had the responsibility for running the trading desk, it would work fine without excess volatility. (See Fisher's statements quoted in Taylor, 2018.) Most likely, the level of reserve balances will be greater than observed in 2006 and depend on liquidity regulations, but the defining concept of a market-determined interest rate is what is important.

I made the practical case for such a framework in Taylor (2018), drawing on my experience and research on the federal funds market before the Global Financial Crisis and on a model of the market (Taylor, 2001). If we went back to that framework, there would be no need for interest on excess reserves. If the central bank wanted to change the short-term interest rate, it would adjust the supply of reserves. The amount of reserves would be set so that the supply and demand for reserves determine the interest rate. The rate thus would be market determined. The central bank could provide liquidity support if it needed to do so in that framework. The key concept is that economic forces in the market for reserves, and for money more broadly, would determine the interest rate.

In contrast, under a system where the supply of reserves remains above the demand, the interest rate is administered through interest on excess reserves. This raises the chances of the central bank using the size and composition of its balance sheet for other purposes besides monetary policy, including credit allocation and even industrial policy, by helping some sectors and not others. In the early days of massive balance sheet operations in the United States, I used the word *mondustrial* to refer to this mixture of monetary policy and industrial policy. In fact, in the years since the Global Financial Crisis, the Fed has purchased mortgage-backed securities, the ECB has purchased corporate bonds, and the BOJ has purchased private equities. Hence, the central bank can morph into a multipurpose institution, which could lead people to raise questions about its independence.

## 1.7   Monetary Policy Harmonization

In concluding this chapter, it is important to point out that the general issues raised here have been discussed by many generations of economists and central bankers. Although the technical issues and governance challenges are changing as technology has developed and markets have globalized, the debates about monetary policy rules versus discretion have important similarities, and there are historical lessons.

Indeed, recent discussions of issues and problems in the international monetary system are analogous to the discussions and debates about exchange rates and capital flows that occurred seven decades ago as "Friedman (1953) famously challenged the generality and accuracy of the indictment of capital flows in Nurkse (1944)," to use the words of Eichengreen (2004, p. 307) in his historical review. Friedman (1953) argued that monetary policy factors were the cause of the exchange rate and capital flow volatility, while Nurkse (1944) argued that destabilizing speculation was the cause.

For Friedman, the answer was an open international monetary system with monetary policy rules and flexible exchange rates; this system would lead to both less volatility of capital flows and more stable exchange rates. For Nurkse, the answer was limits on exchange rate fluctuations and controls on capital flows.

In a recent review of the history, Dellas and Tavlas (2017) emphasize that Friedman's argument in favor of a flexible exchange rate included that the system must be accompanied by domestic monetary rules. The combination would lead to "superior economic performance" compared with fixed exchange rates and discretionary monetary policy. They also write (Dellas and Tavlas, 2017 p. 2) that the "recent proposal of a rules-based international monetary system—based on flexible exchange rates and a Taylor rule for each country—is very much in that spirit and represents a modern rendition of Friedman's views. Under both the Friedman and Taylor proposals, instead of policy coordination among countries there would be *policy harmonization*." (italics added).

Karl Brunner weighed in often on these issues, always tending to stress the importance of monetary factors, the importance of open capital markets, the importance of flexible exchange rates, and the importance of policy rules, both domestically and internationally. In 1980, he put the kinds of ideas that I have discussed here in a broader, institutional perspective. He wrote, "We suffer neither under total ignorance nor do we enjoy full knowledge. Our life moves in a grey zone of partial knowledge and partial ignorance. More particularly, the products emerging from our professional work reveal a wide range of diffuse uncertainty about the detailed response structure of the economy. ... A nonactivist [rules-based] regime emerges under the circumstances ... as the safest strategy. It does not assure us that economic fluctuations will be avoided. But it will assure us that monetary policymaking does not impose additional uncertainties." (See Brunner, 1980, as quoted in Dorn, 2018).

In the next chapter, I consider questions that have been raised about rules-based monetary systems as proposed in this book.

## 1.8 Appendix: Data Definitions and Sources for Policy Variables

This appendix defines the policy variables used in chapter 1, including the policy interest rates and reserve balances on the balance sheets of the Fed, the ECB, the BOJ, and the SNB.

### Reserve Balances

*Federal Reserve System*

Units are millions of dollars, monthly, not seasonally adjusted

RU = Total reserve balances maintained with Federal Reserve banks

https://fred.stlouisfed.org/series/RESBALN

*Bank of Japan (BOJ)*

RJ = BOJ Current Account Balances/Total (c) (F + G)/Amounts outstanding at end of month)

Units are 100 million yen

Name in the Bank of Japan database is

MD08'MACAB2201(BOJ Current Account Balances/Total (c) (F + G)/Amounts outstanding at the end of the month (Plug this into name in and Search by exact series codes)

http://www.stat-search.boj.or.jp/index_en.html (retrieved on August 10, 2017)

*European Central Bank (ECB)*

Units are millions of euros, monthly

RE = Current accounts + Deposit facility

http://sdw.ecb.europa.eu/browseSelection.do?SERIES
_KEY=123.ILM.M.U2.C.L02010.U2.EUR&SERIES_KEY=123
.ILM.M.U2.C.L020200.U2.EUR&node=bbn27&trans=N

*For figure 1.8, weekly data on RE were created by adding weekly series for the CA and DF, which are not subject to the measurement issues described in the text. The weekly data are from the ECB website:*

*CA weekly:*
*http://sdw.ecb.europa.eu/quickview.do?SERIES_KEY=123.ILM
.M.U2.C.L020100.U2.EUR*

*DF weekly:*
*http://sdw.ecb.europa.eu/quickview.do?SERIES_KEY=123.ILM
.M.U2.C.L020200.U2.EUR*

*Swiss National Bank (SNB)*

Reserve balances (RS)

Units are CHF millions, monthly (February 2017 values are shown in parentheses)

RS = SDD + SDF + OSL (547,146.4)

SDD = Sight deposits of domestic banks (472,945.2)

SDF = Sight deposits of foreign banks and institutions (42,013.4)

OSL = Other sight liabilities (32,187.9)

https://data.snb.ch/en/topics/snb#!/cube/snbbipo

## Policy Interest Rates

*Federal Reserve System*

Effective federal funds rate, monthly average

Source: Federal Reserve Bank of St. Louis, FRED

https://fred.stlouisfed.org/series/FEDFUNDS

*Bank of Japan (BOJ)*

Call rate, uncollateralized, overnight average, monthly

Source: BOJ's Main Time Series Statistics

https://www.stat-search.boj.or.jp/ssi/mtshtml/fm02_m_1
_en.html

*European Central Bank (ECB)*

Interest rate on DF, monthly

Source: ECB's Financial Market Data

https://sdw.ecb.europa.eu/quickview.do?SERIES_KEY
=143.FM.B.U2.EUR.4F.KR.DFR.LEV

*Swiss National Bank (SNB)*

Swiss Average Rate Overnight (SARON)

Source: SNB, Money market rates

https://data.snb.ch/en/topics/ziredev#!/cube/zimoma

**Exchange Rates**

The six bilateral exchange rate series are as follows:

XJU, yen per 1 dollar

XJE, yen per 1 euro

XUE, dollars per 1 euro

XSU, Swiss francs per 1 dollar

XSE, Swiss francs per 1 euro

XSJ, Swiss francs per 1 yen

Source: https://fred.stlouisfed.org/.

# 2 Deep Questions about Rules-Based Monetary Policy

At the core of the international monetary reform proposed in the previous chapter is a rules-based system at each central bank. The idea of monetary policy rules has been around for a long time in economics, but research and practical policy applications have exploded in recent years. This chapter reviews the state of the debate over rules versus discretion in monetary policy, focusing on the role of economic research in this debate. It shows that proposals for policy rules were not pulled out of thin air, but rather were largely based on empirical research using economic models. Frequently, the models are international, involving two or more countries.

These models demonstrate the advantages of a systematic approach to monetary policy, although proposed rules have changed and generally improved over time. Rules derived from research help central bankers formulate monetary policy as they operate in both domestic financial markets and the international monetary system. However, the line of demarcation between rules and discretion is difficult to establish in practice, which makes contrasting the two approaches difficult. History shows that research on policy rules has had an impact on the practice of central banking in many countries. Economic research also shows that while central bank independence is crucial for good monetary policymaking, it has not been enough to prevent swings away from rules-based policy, implying that policymakers might consider enhanced reporting about how rules are used in monetary policy. This chapter also explores the fact that during the past year and a half, there has been a refocus on policy rules in implementing monetary policy in the United States, and this may be spreading to other countries in the international monetary system.

I organize the chapter into sections based on a question-and-answer format. The questions delve into (1) changes in suggested policy rules over time, (2) the idea of tying the hands of central bankers, (3) the difficulty of demarcating discretion, (4) the influence of policy-rule research on the practice of central banking, and (5) the purpose of recently proposed legislation on monetary strategies.

## 2.1   How Have the Various Rules Suggested for Monetary Policy Changed over Time?

In addressing this question, it is important to note first that economists have been suggesting monetary policy rules from the beginning. Adam Smith (1776) argued in *The Wealth of Nations (p. 335)* that "a well-regulated paper-money" could improve economic growth and stability, as opposed to a pure commodity standard, as discussed by Asso and Leeson (2012). Henry Thornton wrote in 1802 that a central bank should have the responsibility for price level stability and should make the mechanism explicit and "not be a matter of ongoing discretion," as Robert Hetzel (1987, p. 15) put it. David Ricardo (1824, pp. 10–11) wrote in his *Plan for the Establishment of a National Bank* that government ministers "could not be safely entrusted with the power of issuing paper money," and advanced the idea of a rule-guided central bank. In the early 20th century, Knut Wicksell (1907) and Irving Fisher (1920) proposed policy rules for the interest rate or the money supply to avoid the kinds of monetary-induced disturbances that led to hyperinflation or depression. Henry Simons (1936) and Milton Friedman (1948) continued in that tradition, recognizing that monetary policy rules—such as a constant growth rate rule for the money supply—would avoid such mistakes in contrast with discretion.

The goal of these reformers was a monetary system that prevented monetary shocks and cushioned the economy from other shocks, thereby reducing the chances of inflation, financial crises, and recession. Their idea was that a simple monetary rule with little discretion could avoid monetary excesses, whether due to government deficits, commodity discoveries, or mistakes by government. The choice was often broader than the modern distinction of rules versus discretion, as explained in Taylor and Williams (2011); it was "rules versus chaotic monetary policy," whether the chaos was caused by policymakers' discretion or simply exogenous shocks like gold discoveries or shortages.

Over time, economic research on monetary policy rules has expanded greatly and the design of rules has improved. While international factors have always been key consideration in the design of policy rules, the models have become more international as the world has become more integrated financially, and the concerns of small, open, emerging-market economies have received increased attention. To understand and appreciate how the suggestions for policy rules have changed, it is necessary to examine the changes in econometric models used to design rules. Moreover, a brief historical review of how policy evaluation methodology and research have developed offers important insights.

Recall that the first macroeconomic model, built in 1936 by Jan Tinbergen (1959), was designed to answer a monetary policy question involving key international monetary issues— namely, whether the devaluation of a currency of a small, open economy would stimulate that economy. The currency was the guilder, the country was the Netherlands, and the model was of the Dutch economy. The model had thirty-two stochastic equations and was based on the ideas of John Maynard Keynes. To answer the question, Tinbergen simulated the model and examined how a change in the *policy instrument*—the exchange rate—affected the *target variables*— employment and output. Soon after the paper was circulated, the guilder was devalued by about 20 percent (in September 1936), suggesting that the econometric model influenced that decision.

Tinbergen's model-based simulations of instruments and targets put economists and statisticians onto a new line of research: building, estimating, and simulating policy models. The common framework involved calculating the impact of alternative paths for policy instruments on target variables, which stimulated research on structural models in the 1940s and 1950s at the Cowles Commission and Foundation. Lawrence Klein took the research further in the 1950s by building more complex models.

After a considerable lag, the research staffs of central banks began to adopt these models and this approach to policy evaluation, sometimes in collaboration with academics. In the 1960s, the MIT-PENN-SSRC (MPS) model with seventy-five stochastic equations was adopted for use by the Federal Reserve (Fed). Papers by de Leeuw and Gramlich (1968) and Ando and Rasche (1971) tell this story, and it was the same situation at many other central banks. For example, in the 1960s, the RDX1 model (and then RDX2 and RDXF models) was were developed at the Bank of Canada, as described by Helliwell, Officer, Shapiro, and Stewart (1969).

After a few years—about halfway through this eight-decade history—there was a major paradigm shift. Views changed about how models should be used to evaluate monetary policy. It was a shift from policy evaluation in *path-space* to policy evaluation in *rule-space*. In path-space, one uses an econometric model to estimate the impact of a one-time change in the path of the policy instrument on the target variables. In rule-space, one estimates the impact of a policy rule for the instruments on the dynamic stochastic properties of the target variables. I reviewed the shift and used this terminology in talks at the Dutch National Bank (September 29, 2016), the Bank of Canada (November 17, 2016), and the Bank of Korea (May 10, 2017).

The shift had many antecedents. One was the realization that Milton Friedman's arguments regarding predictability and accountability applied to steady feedback rules as well as to the constant money growth rate rules. Moreover, it was discovered that a natural way to evaluate policy in the new dynamic or stochastic models of the economy was by simulating policy rules. This is how engineers had been designing servomechanisms to stabilize dynamic stochastic systems. The early work by A. W. Phillips (1954) on proportional, derivative, and integral control is an example. Another factor leading to analysis with rules is that they simplified difficult problems such as joint estimation and control, as shown by Anderson and Taylor (1976). In addition, newer rational expectations models led to serious critiques by Lucas (1976) and Kydland and Prescott (1977) of conventional path-space approaches. Moreover, the incorporation of sticky wage and price dynamics into these forward-looking models meant that many of the problems confronting monetary policymakers could be approached by monetary policy rules rather than by one-time changes in the policy instrument.

Difficult computational tasks with the larger and frequently international rational expectations models needed by central banks created a significant barrier, but algorithms and computers soon improved, and change eventually happened. The Brookings Model Comparison program in the late 1980s and early 1990s helped. In Bryant, Hooper, and Mann (1993), I noted the change, saying that "[w]hereas previous model-comparison exercises conducted by the Brookings Institution have looked at the effects on the economy of one-time changes in the instruments of monetary and fiscal policy—that is, *policy multipliers*—this exercise has emphasized comparisons of the response of the economy to monetary policy regimes that are simplified *policy rules*."(p. 426) So, in the early 1990s, the MPS model at the Fed was replaced by the FRB/U.S. model. As stated by Brayton and Tinsley (1996), in the FRB/U.S model, "expectations of private sectors are explicit, and these expectations, especially market perceptions of policy, constitute a major transmission channel of monetary policy." Brayton, Levin, Tryon, and Williams (1997) provide a good history of this development.

The same change was underway at other central banks, including those in smaller open economies. In the early 1990s, the Bank of Canada replaced the RDXF model with the Quarterly Projection Model (QPM). In their exposition of the new model, Poloz, Rose, and Tetlow (1994, p 26)) emphasized the computational challenges of solving models with rational or "model-consistent" expectations, noting that they relied on an iterative method for "solving forward-looking models [that] was developed by R. Fair and J. Taylor (1983)." Coletti, Hunt, Rose, and Tetlow (1996) noted that the "two important features of that dynamic structure [of the QPM] are forward-looking expectations and endogenous policy rules." (p. 26) This modeling framework continued through the 1990s and into the 2000s at the Bank of Canada as a new dynamic model with rational expectations and sticky prices, called the Terms-of-Trade Economic Model (ToTEM), replaced the QPM. Computation speeds and solution algorithms also have improved greatly (Maliar, Maliar, Taylor, and Tsener, 2015).

Volker Wieland's macro model database (MMB) provides a broader perspective on this change in monetary policy research by including models at other central banks and by tracing developments over time. Wieland, Afanasyeva, Kuete, and Yoo (2016) classified models into first-, second-, and third-generation new Keynesian models. While these models differed in structure, there was a surprising amount of consensus in what they implied about the impact of monetary policy rules on the economy, as shown by Taylor and Wieland (2012).

As with earlier research, the main policy objective was to find monetary policy rules that cushioned the economy from shocks and did not cause their own shocks. But the models were getting complex, and thus the policy rules were getting complex, and this raised serious doubts about the practical applicability of the whole rule-space framework. The question then became whether simple practical rules consistent with the economic models could be found. The answer turned out to be "yes," and this led to a huge change in the type of policy rules suggested for monetary policy.

It turned out that the rules by which the policy interest rate reacted to real gross domestic product (GDP) and inflation worked well in these models. Research showed that the interest rate reaction to inflation should be greater than 1, the interest rate reaction to the GDP gap should be greater than 0, and the interest rate reaction to other variables should be small. For the Taylor (1993a) rule, the inflation target was 2 percent (taking into account inflation measurement bias and the zero lower bound on the interest rate), and the equilibrium interest rate was 2 percent in real terms and 4 percent in nominal terms. While some argue that the inflation target should be raised above 2 percent in light of their estimates that the equilibrium rate is now lower, the rule was not the result of a curve-fitting exercise in which various instruments of policy were regressed on other variables. This simple rule was derived from first-generation policy models operating in rule-space.

To this day, people say that such rules are too simple because they omit certain variables. Well, they *were* simple, because they were *made to be simple*. At the time, people were coming up with all sorts of complex rules that included many types of variables, including asset prices. These rules were too complex to be workable in practice. It was amazing that they could be simplified. Rules from which certain variables were removed gave an equally good performance in many models as more complex rules. Simple rules were more robust than optimal rules over a wide range of models, and they were certainly more practical for policymakers to work with.

Levin and Williams (2003) and Orphanides and Williams (2008) found that more complex, fully optimal policies performed poorly in some models, while simple rules performed well in a wide variety of models. Optimal policies can be overly fine-tuned to a specific model. That is fine if that model is correct, but not if it is incorrect. Simple monetary policy rules incorporated basic principles such as leaning against the wind of inflation and output. Because they were not fine-tuned to specific assumptions, they were more robust.

The new rules that were suggested led in other directions, which helped to reinforce their use. Economists learned that policy rules helped them explain unusual phenomena, such as the positive correlation between inflation surprises and exchange rate movements (Engel and West, 2006). Interest in policy rules also grew beyond academia and central banks: Wall Street economists found them to be useful rules of thumb for predicting central bank actions, as explained by Lipsky (2012). Also, policy rules affected other equations in models because with them, it became more reasonable to assume that economic agents develop their own rules of thumb when monetary policy becomes more predictable. And it enabled economists to consider policy robustness in a rigorous way, as emphasized by McCallum (1999), and continued today, as reviewed by Wieland et al. (2016).

The rule-space approach was applied internationally (Taylor, 1993b). As discussed earlier in chapter 1, research with international models demonstrated the near-global optimality in rule-space of a Nash equilibrium, in which each central bank followed an optimal policy for its country assuming that other central banks would do the same. Thus, the research showed that rule-based monetary policy would lead to good macroeconomic performance in the national economy and the global economy. This in turn has led to suggestions for designing a rules-based international monetary system based on policy rules in each country (Taylor, 2016b).

The fact that the simple rules appeared to work well in practice also helped to reinforce confidence in the rules that were being suggested. Central banks in many countries appeared to be moving toward more transparent rules-based policies in the 1980s and 1990s, including through a focus on price stability, and economic performance improved. This connection between the rules-based policy and performance was detected by Taylor (1998b) and by Clarida, Gali, and Gertler (2000). There was an especially dramatic improvement compared with the 1970s, when policy was highly discretionary, and the models were used in a path-space mode. Mervyn King (2003) called it the NICE period (with *NICE* standing for "noninflationary consistently expansionary"), and there was also a near-internationally cooperative equilibrium (another *NICE*) among most developed countries, as there were few complaints about spillovers. By 2000, many emerging-market countries adopted the rules-based policy approach, usually through inflation targeting. Their improved performance contributed to global stability.

Unfortunately, it did not last. The Great Moderation ended, and the Global Financial Crisis arrived. There has been debate about why the better performance ended, and this has led to further debate and suggested additional changes in policy rules. I have argued that the Fed turned away from the policy rule that had been working well. The departure began before the crisis, when interest rates were set too low for too long. Kahn (2010) and Ahrend (2010) have provided evidence of monetary policy swinging away from rule-like policies. Kohn (2012) questioned using simple policy rules to make that judgment. More recently, Lane (2016) cites evidence in an IMF Staff Report (2015) that both "macroeconomic gaps" and "financial gaps" (Lane 2016, chart 1, p. 5.) were large in several countries, suggesting that interest rates should not have been so low.

As discussed in chapter 1, Hofmann and Bogdanova (2012) show that there has been a "Global Great Deviation" from policy rules, and one reason why the deviation became global is that central banks followed each other. In many countries, estimated central bank reaction functions have a significant coefficient on foreign policy rates or on deviations from rules-based policy in other countries (Gray, 2013; Carstens, 2015; Edwards, 2017).

While there is an issue of causality versus correlation, econometric and historical evidence points to a close temporal connection between this deviation in policy and deteriorating performance. Following the Global Great Deviation, NICE ended in both senses of the word. Nikolsko-Rzhevskyy, Papell, and Prodan (2014) provide econometric evidence for the United States, and Teryoshin (2017) does the same for nine countries, including the United States. Allan Meltzer (2012) provides historical evidence that the change in policy led to a and the change in performance There are also concerns about international spillover effects, and emerging-market countries have been affected by increased exchange rates and capital flow volatility.

The other view, expressed for example by the central bankers King (2012) and Carney (2013), is that the onset of poor economic performance was not due to a deviation from policy rules that were working, but rather to other factors. They illustrated the concept with the Taylor frontier or curve (Taylor, 1979b), as Bernanke (2004) did earlier to illustrate the effects of change in policy versus change in structure of the economy. Carney (2013), for example, argued that the deterioration of performance in recent years occurred because "the disruptive potential of financial instability—absent effective macroprudential policies—leads to a less favourable Taylor frontier." (p. 23) The Taylor curve used by Bernanke, Carney, and King is shown in figure 2.1, as drawn directly from Carney (2013), though he and King reverse the axis labels compared with Bernanke (2004) and Taylor (1979).

The variance of output and the variance of inflation are on the axes, representing the goals of price and output stability. Better outcomes are shown down and to the left in the graph. The Carney-King view is that performance deteriorated from point A to point B in the diagram because the

Variance of inflation

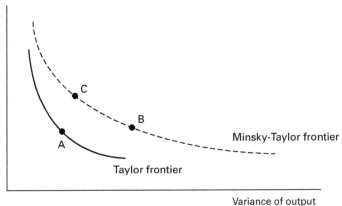
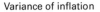

**Figure 2.1**
Bernanke-Carney-King illustration of good or bad policy using the Taylor curve. *Source*: Carney (2013), King (2012).

Taylor curve shifted to what they call the *Minsky-Taylor curve*, conveying Hyman Minsky's idea that financial stability breeds instability as markets become complacent. My view is that the deterioration from A to B was due to a move away from the Taylor curve caused by a change in monetary policy, rather than to a shift in the curve due to nonmonetary factors. That view would suggest moving back toward the type of policy rule that described policy decisions during the Great Moderation period, as represented by point A. Bernanke (2004) agreed with me that an earlier move from B to A was due to a change in monetary policy, though his views about the move back from A to B were that it was due to nonmonetary policy factors, similar to the view of Carney and King.

In any case, this experience led to more suggestions for changes in policy rules. There has been a great deal of renewed interest in nominal GDP targeting, as suggested by Sumner

(2014). Beckworth and Hendrickson (2015), for example, have examined interest rate rules where the central bank reacts to nominal GDP, rather than to the inflation rate and GDP separately. They stress that such a rule has the advantage that the central bank does not have to estimate potential GDP, reflecting concerns raised by Orphanides (2003).

Another way in which the suggested rules are changing over time is the reconsideration of money growth rules. Belongia and Ireland (2014) show that the Divisia index of the money supply has effects on the economy over and above the effects of the short-term interest rate. Their research suggests that central bankers should consider money growth rate rules. Another example is given by Fagan, Lothian, and McNelis (2013), who examine monetary rules for the monetary base. In my early work on policy rules in the 1970s, I began by suggesting money growth rules, but the models showed that interest rates rules would work better, at least with the range of shocks observed in the United States. Nevertheless, I argued that interest rate rules need to be placed within a band: Outside that band, the central bank should rely on money growth rules. In situations where the interest rate hits the lower bound, I have argued that central banks need to focus on a policy rule that keeps the growth rate of the money supply steady. In Taylor (1996), for example, I recommended that "[i]nterest rate rules need to be supplemented by money supply rules in cases of either extended deflation or hyperinflation." (p. 37)

Another suggestion is to use forecasts of variables in the policy rule rather than actual values. If that is not done, then people say that a rule is not forward-looking because it includes current variables rather than forecasts of those variables. But the Taylor (1993a) rule, for example, was designed to deal explicitly with forward-looking agents, and therefore, it is forward-looking itself. Note that when a central bank indicates that it will predictably follow a strategy in which the interest rate reacts to the current inflation rate, it automatically says that the next period's interest rate will react to the next period's inflation rate. That's forward-looking. Moreover, the current level of inflation and output are key factors in any forecast of inflation, and the coefficients of existing policy rules take that into account. If one replaced current inflation with a forecast of inflation, the coefficients most likely have to be different. And the approach raises the question of whose forecast to use and how to evaluate the rule. Forecasts—including central bank forecasts—are not always that good. Also, rules with forecasts of inflation and output on the right side tend to be less robust.

Other suggested changes in policy rules in recent years are due to the effective lower bound (ELB) on the interest rate, which was reached during and after the crisis. At minimum, the standard monetary policy rule should be truncated to account for the ELB. But the ELB also has other implications for the design of the monetary policy rule. Reifschneider and Williams (2000) find that increasing the response to the output gap helps reduce the effects of the ELB. However, this could increase the variability of inflation and interest rates.

Reifschneider and Williams (2000) also suggested other changes. In one suggestion, the policy rule is modified to lower the interest rate more aggressively than it otherwise would be when close to the ELB—for example, by cutting the interest rate to zero if the unconstrained interest rate falls below 1 percent. This adds monetary stimulus near the ELB, which can offset the constraining effects when the ELB hits.

In a second suggestion, the interest rate is kept extra low following an ELB incident; for example, the interest rate is kept at zero until the absolute value of the cumulative sum of negative deviations of the actual interest rate from the ELB equals what occurred during the period of that ELB. These approaches mitigate the effects of the ELB according to model simulations. This suggestion is a form of forward guidance, and more generally, such communication about future interest rate changes is a frequently suggested change in monetary policy rules in recent years. However, forward guidance should be consistent with the policy rule or strategy of the central bank. If it is purposely meant to promise interest rates in the future that are inconsistent with the strategy, then it is time-inconsistent, which leads to uncertainty and confusion. If forward guidance is consistent with the policy strategy, then it is simply a matter of being transparent about the strategy. Frequent changes in forward guidance cause problems for monetary policy.

Another recent suggested change in policy rules is to adopt a price-level target rather than an inflation target. Reifschneider and Williams (2000) find that such price-level targeting rules reduce the costs of the ELB. As with their second suggested policy rule, it promises more monetary stimulus than a standard inflation-targeting policy rule. This anticipation of lower rates in the future boosts the economy even when it is at the ELB.

It is worth noting that the ELB was not a reason to deviate from rules-based policy in 2003–2005 because even the zero lower bound was not binding.[5] The zero bound appears to have been binding in 2009, but by then, suggestions based on the research of Reifshneider and Williams (2000) were available and were being widely discussed.

Another suggested change in policy rules, motivated in part by the ELB, is a higher target inflation rate. If the target inflation rate is sufficiently high, the ELB will rarely constrain monetary policy and the macroeconomy. In the past, a 2 percent inflation target was viewed as sufficient to avoid these constraints; that is why 2 percent is close to the inflation target of many central banks today, but that view has been questioned recently.

Looking toward the future, changes in technology are likely to affect suggestions for policy rules. The advent of sophisticated nowcasting has mitigated the limitation that central bankers do not know much about the current quarter. And the development of digital currency may enable central banks to have a wider range of flexibility in setting the policy instruments, as discussed by Bordo and Levin (2017).

Perhaps the most important suggested change in policy rules in recent years is to adjust the intercept to accommodate the lower estimate of the equilibrium real interest rate ($r^*$). For example, in the Taylor rule, the equilibrium real interest rate was set to 2 percent, meaning that with the 2 percent target inflation rate in the rule, the equilibrium nominal rate would be 4 percent. But according to members of the FOMC, the average estimate is at least 1 percentage point lower now. Laubach and Williams (2003, 2016) have provided evidence for this, and Holston, Laubach, and Williams (2016) examine the effect internationally. Taylor and Weiland (2016) have shown there is a great deal of uncertainty about the estimates and that the low interest rates set by central banks make it even more difficult to estimate the equilibrium real rate. In any case, aside from this uncertainty, there is no reason why a moving equilibrium rate could not be incorporated into policy rules in different countries, as the Bank for International Settlements (BIS) did in creating the policy rules reported in figure 1.1 of chapter 1. Debates about the implications of changes in the equilibrium interest rate are more productive if they are conducted within the framework of a policy rule rather than in the abstract.

## 2.2   Have the Reasons Given for Why We Might Want to Tie a Central Banker's Hands Evolved?

Several years ago, I was asked to list the reasons for a rules-based approach rather than a discretionary approach to monetary policy, and I did so in Taylor (1998a). Similar views were expressed by McCallum (1999) and Taylor and Williams (2011). Although I would not characterize this list as reasons why we might want to tie central bankers' hands, they are nonetheless reasons why central banks would want to choose to run monetary policy in a rule-like fashion:

**1. Preventing time inconsistency.** The time inconsistency problem calls for using a policy rule in order to reduce the chance that the monetary policymakers will change their policy after people in the private sector have taken their actions.

**2. Clearer explanations.** If a policy rule is simple, it can make explaining monetary policy decisions to the public or to students of public policy much easier. It is difficult to explain why a specific interest rate is being chosen at a specific date without reference to a method or procedure such as would be described by a policy rule. The use of a policy rule can mean a better-educated public and a more effective democracy. It also can help to take some of the mystique out of monetary policy.

**3. Less short-run political pressure.** Policy rules are less subject to political pressure than discretionary policy. If monetary policy appears to be run in an ad hoc way rather than a systematic way, then politicians may argue that they can be just as ad hoc and interfere with monetary policy decisions. A monetary policy rule that shows how the instruments of policy must be set in a large number of circumstances is less subject to political pressure every time conditions change.

**4. Reducing uncertainty.** Policy rules reduce uncertainty by providing guidance about future policy actions. The use of monetary policy rules by financial analysts as an aid in forecasting actual changes in the instruments reduces uncertainty in the financial markets.

**5. Teaching the art and science of central banking.** Monetary policy rules are a good way to instruct new central bankers in the art and science of monetary policy. In fact, it is for exactly this reason that new central bankers frequently find such policy rules useful for assessing their decisions.

**6. Greater accountability.** Policy rules for instrument settings lead to more accountability by policymakers. Because monetary policy works with a long and variable lag, it is difficult to determine if policymakers are doing a good job simply by looking at inflation. Today's inflation rate depends on past decisions, but today's settings for the instruments of policy—the monetary base and the short-term nominal interest rate—depend on today's decisions.

**7. A useful historical benchmark.** Policy rules provide a useful baseline for historical comparison. For example, if the interest rate was at a certain level at a time in the past with similar macroeconomic conditions to those of today, then that same level would be a good baseline from which to consider today's policy actions.

Of course, there are also technical reasons for rules, such as the fact that the economy is a dynamic stochastic evolving entity and requires analysis in the rule-space, as discussed in the previous section. And there are also political reasons: Like the rule of law, a predictable policy that applies without exception preserves individual freedom. But the list of seven is most relevant to the question of whether a rules-based system can be used in practice.

Many of the reasons would be the same if the word *strategy* were used rather than *policy rule,* and if we were referring to any other policy than monetary policy. It is not that we want to tie central bankers' hands as much as we want a policy that works well, and that is the case when a clear strategy is in place. George Shultz (2014) explained the importance of having a strategy, writing that "it is important, based on my own experience, to have a rules-based monetary policy. ... At least as I have observed from policy decisions over the years in various fields, if you have a strategy, you get somewhere. If you don't have a strategy, you are just a tactician at large and it doesn't add up." (p. 142)

A related point is that having a policy rule or strategy does not mean that a policymaker can't do things that need to be done. Any reasonable law enforcement strategy will require actions by law enforcement officials. And sometimes not acting amounts to violating a strategy: For example, a decision by government financial regulators to refrain from acting when an institution takes on risk beyond the limits of the regulations in place is inaction, and clearly poor policy. Policymakers need to explain that a policy strategy involves a series of actions.

In my view, the reasons *for* monetary policy rules stated here have not evolved much over the years. However, the reasons *against* policy rules have evolved, and so they deserve some discussion in this assessment. They are sometimes characterized as why we should not tie central bankers' hands.

At the 2013 American Economic Association meetings, Larry Summers and I had a debate about rules versus discretion. The transcript was later published in the *Journal of Policy*

*Modeling,*[6] and I quote from that here. Summers (2014, p. 697) started by saying: "John Taylor and I have, it will not surprise you ... a fundamental philosophical difference, and I would put it in this way. I think about my doctor. Which would I prefer: for my doctor's advice to be consistently predictable, or for my doctor's advice to be responsive to the medical condition with which I present? Me, I'd rather have a doctor who most of the time didn't tell me to take some stuff, and every once in a while said I needed to ingest some stuff into my body in response to the particular problem that I had. That would be a doctor [whose advice], believe me, would be less predictable."

Thus, Summers argues in favor of relying on an all-knowing expert—for instance, a doctor who does not perceive the need for, and does not use, a set of guidelines, but who once in a while, in an unpredictable way, says to ingest some stuff. I would describe modern medical practice differently than Summers, emphasizing that in medicine, as in economics, there has been progress over the years. And much progress has been due to doctors using rules, or what they call checklists, as described by Atul Gawande (2007). Of course, doctors need to exercise judgment in implementing checklists, but if they start winging it or skipping steps, patients usually suffer. Experience and empirical studies show that checklist-free medicine is fraught with danger, just as rules-free, strategy-free monetary policy is.

Another recent development also appears as an argument for not wanting to tie the hands of decision-makers. At a recent Brookings conference, Ben Bernanke (2015) argued that the Fed had been following a policy rule, including during the "too low for too long" period. But the rule that Bernanke had in mind is not a rule in the sense that I have used it in this discussion, or in the way that many others have used it.

Rather, it is a concept that all you really need for effective policymaking is a goal, such as an inflation target or an employment target. In medicine, it would be the goal of keeping patients healthy. The rest of policymaking is doing whatever you as an expert, or you as an expert with models, thinks needs to be done with the instruments. You do not need to articulate or describe a strategy, a decision rule, or a contingency plan for the instruments. If you want to hold the interest rate well below the rule-based strategy that worked well during the Great Moderation, as the Fed did in 2003–2005, then that's OK if you can justify it in terms of the goal that you want to reach.

Bernanke (2003) argued in a speech before the Money Marketeers of New York University that this approach is a form of "constrained discretion." It is an appealing term, and it may be constraining discretion in some sense, but it does not induce or encourage a rule, as these words would have you believe. Simply having a specific numerical goal or objective function is not a rule for the instruments of policy, and it is not a strategy; in my view, it ends up being all tactics. I think that there is evidence that relying solely on constrained discretion has not worked for monetary policy.

Another evolution of the policy rule concept is also related to concerns about tying central bankers' hands. This is the idea of "inflation forecast targeting," or simply "forecast targeting," as developed by Svensson (1998) and Woodford (2012). Indeed, Svensson entitled his 1998 paper "Inflation Forecast Targeting: Implementing and Monitoring Inflation Targets" emphasizing the practical nature of idea, and Woodford entitled his 2012 paper "Forecast Targeting as a Monetary Policy Strategy," emphasizing that this alternative approach is a strategy. There is a close connection between "inflation forecast targeting" or "inflation targeting" and policy rules for the instruments. In Taylor (2012a), I argued that they were the dual solution to the same problem, much as first-order conditions and decision rules provide dual and complementary answers to the same optimization problem. One can learn from both approaches.

According to this approach, the central bank chooses its policy interest rate so that a linear combination of its forecast of different variables would fall along a given path. Woodford (2012) suggested that a linear combination of the $h$-period forecast ahead of the inflation rate $\pi_{t+h,t}$ relative to the target inflation rate $\pi^*$, and the $h$-period forecast ahead of the output gap $x_{t+h,t}$ follows the path $(\pi_{t+h,t}-\pi^*)+\varphi x_{t+h,t}=0$ over a range of $h$, where interest rate policy can affect these variables.

While an interest rate path can be calculated using this approach, it need not yield a simple policy rule for the instruments. The central bank would have the job of deciding on the instrument setting, and this might cause tension with some of the reasons for policy rules given in this discussion. Qvigstad (2005) showed how charts and other diagnostic tests could be used to describe the intended path for the interest rate. In addition, with examples from policy decisions by the Norges Bank, he showed how policy rules could be used as a cross-check, emphasizing the connection between proposals for policy rules for the instruments and forecast targeting.

Although this book is focused on monetary policy rules, not on other activities of central banks, such as being the lender of last resort and financial supervision and regulation, it is appropriate to mention, as discussed further in Taylor (2016a), that economic research implies that there are reasons to limit the scope of a central bank. In granting independence to a government agency in a democracy, one needs to make sure that the agency has a well-defined limited purpose, with strong accountability.

When central banks drift too far from being limited-purpose institutions and become independent multipurpose institutions, they escape the checks and balances needed in a democratic system. This can lead to inappropriate interventions that may not have been approved by a legislative process or a vote of the people. It can also lead to poor economic performance. Research shows that central bank independence is necessary for good monetary policy, and thus good macroeconomic performance, but it is not sufficient.

## 2.3    What Is the Line Demarcating Rules-Based Policy and a Discretionary Policy?

The question "What is the line between rules-based policy and discretionary policy?" is fundamental and highly practical. McCallum (1999) devoted the first section of his comprehensive review of monetary rules to the distinction between rules and discretion, admitting, "When it comes to practical application to the behavior of actual central banks, however, the distinction cannot be easily drawn." (p. 1487). He argued that in my paper "Discretion Versus Policy Rules in Practice" (Taylor, 1993a), I "explicitly addressed the problem" (p. 1487) by saying that rule-like behavior is systematic in the sense of "methodical, according to plan, and not casual or at random." (p. 213). Indeed, the stated purpose of that paper was "to study the role of policy rules in a world where simple, algebraic formulations of such rules cannot and should not be mechanically followed by policymakers."

I elaborated on the demarcation later (Taylor, 2012b, p. 1018):

When assessing in practice whether monetary policy is rules-based, it is not necessary to focus on purely theoretical definitions of rules versus discretion—such as might come out of game theory or the time-inconsistency literature, where policy is at one extreme or the other. Nor is it necessary to limit the definition of rules-based policy to situations where the policy instruments are set perfectly in line with an algebraic formula. Rather, the distinction between rules and discretion is more a matter of degree. There are several ways to assess and measure whether monetary policy is more rules-based or less rules-based.

When monetary policy is rules-based, decisions about the policy instruments are more predictable and more systematic. Policymakers can and do discuss their strategy in dynamic terms, including the implications of a decision today for decisions in the future. They tend to use formulas or equations for the policy instruments, at least as a guide when making decisions. And their decisions about the policy instruments can be described reasonably well by a stable relationship, which shows a consistent reaction of the policy instruments to observable events such as changes in inflation and real economic growth.

In contrast, in the case of more discretionary policy making, decisions are less predictable and more ad hoc, and they tend to focus on short-term fine-tuning. Policymakers show little interest in coming to agreement about an overall contingency strategy for setting the instruments of policy, and the historical paths for the instruments are not well described by stable algebraic relationships.

It was by using this definition that I found that the period from 1985 to 2003 was rule-like, while the years before and after that interval were discretionary. As already noted, economic performance was far better in the 1985–2003 period. Using an historical approach, Meltzer (2012) also identified the years from 1985 through 2003 as being rules-based rather than discretionary, and he noted that this was also a period of relatively good economic performance.

To apply more rigorous statistical tests to the rules versus discretion issue, Nikolsko-Rzhevskyy et al. (2014) and Teryoshin (2017) have had to be more specific and directly face the questions addressed here. In evaluating rules versus discretion, Nikolsko-Rzhevskyy et al. (2014) decided to consider well-known policy rules—similar to the Taylor rule—as the definition of rule-based policy, and deviations from that as the demarcation of discretion. As Teryoshin (2017), who followed a similar approach in the United States and other countries, puts it, he calculated "the absolute deviation between the policy-rule recommendation using real-time data and the actual central bank rate. Higher values are times of greater discretion relative to the rule, while smaller values suggest a more rule-like monetary policy." (p. 8)

In this way, they provided a more formal statistical foundation for the results of Meltzer (2012) and Taylor (2012b). These papers used various statistical techniques to determine when in history monetary policy was rule-like, and they showed that the rule-like periods coincide remarkably well with periods of good economic performance. By taking a stand and measuring deviations from policy rules, Nikolsko-Rzhevskyy et al. (2014) made an important contribution to the large body of empirical literature on policy rules. Teryoshin (2017) established the robustness of those results and usefully extended the analysis to other countries using data available to policymakers at the time. A difficulty with this approach, of course, is that the definition of discretion depends on the policy rule.

It would be possible to envisage, as an alternative, a complicated rule that fits the data very well, where discretion would therefore be very small and where the periods of rule-like performance are quite different. For example, if you put in a lagged dependent variable (interest rate) into the policy rule—as with an inertial rule—you would have smaller deviations. In reality, one cannot usually distinguish between lagged dependent variables and serially correlated errors, so the lags will be there. By putting in a lagged dependent variable, the econometrician is effectively saying, "Policy is good now, and if it moves just a little bit, it's still pretty good," even though it may be bad, based on the rule without inertia.

Dotsey (2016) argues that the so-called optimal policy rule also would have inertia terms, as in Giannoni and Woodford (2005), so it is not just an arbitrary lagged dependent variable. The optimal policy approach uses an intertemporal optimization problem. In Giannoni and Woodford (2005), the optimal policy can be written as a single equation in terms of leads and lags of the objective variables, such as inflation and output. An advantage of the optimal policy approach over simple monetary policy rules is that it incorporates all relevant information. However, this informational advantage has been found to be surprisingly small in model simulations, even when the central bank is assumed to have perfect knowledge of the model. Williams (2003) used the FRB/U.S. model, and he found that a simple policy rule gives outcomes close to those with the optimal policy.

A related complication is that monetary policy may not follow a rule, but it may seem to have a systematic component, in the sense that there are small deviations from that component with small effect, as Ramey (2016) shows. In some cases, these are deviations from vector autoregressions that may combine rule-like and discretionary regimes. In other cases, the systematic part may be based on a narrative that does not define regime changes as has been done here. In either case, the results indicate the importance of extending existing results to a wider array of policy rules.

Another issue is that deviations from policy rules can be designed to be rule-like in ways that the econometrician does not know. The adjustment to the interest rate that I suggested in Taylor (2008) presents an example of how a seemingly discretionary development can be incorporated into a policy rule in a systematic way. At that time, my research suggested that there was increased counterparty risk among banks, related to concerns about securities derived from subprime mortgages. Based on this research, I testified in Congress that as a first line of defense, central banks should reduce their policy interest rate by the increased spread between LIBOR and the overnight index swap (OIS), which was about 50 basis points at the time, and then do more research to find the reasons for the higher credit risk. This adjustment is an example of why the Taylor rule should not be used mechanically, as I emphasized in the original Taylor rule paper (Taylor, 1993a), but the adjustment was meant to deal in a systematic way with a problem in the money market when the spread between LIBOR and OIS widened significantly. I argued that the models that were used to find the Taylor rule in the first place implied such an adjustment.

## 2.4   How Is the Practice of Central Banking Being Influenced by Debate on Rules-Based Policy?

In the first section of this chapter, I showed how suggestions for policy rules have changed over time, and that swings toward and away from rules-based policy are usually associated with swings in economic performance. The question that I address in this section is how the research on optimal monetary policy rules and the resulting suggestions *directly* affect the analysis and decisions of monetary policymakers and their committees. The question is difficult to answer, although increased central bank transparency will aid future investigations.

Kahn (2012) provides much useful detail about how policy rules have been the subject of discussion at the Fed, using transcripts and records of the Federal Open Market Committee

(FOMC) meetings starting in the 1990s. He also considers the proceedings at other central banks, including the European Central Bank (ECB), the Bank of Japan (BOJ), and the Bank of England. When I first read Kahn's paper, I was surprised to see a great deal of discussion related to policy rules through the 1990s. For example, Janet Yellen referred to the Taylor rule in the FOMC transcripts in 1995. This corresponds to the time period when actual policy decisions were rule-like. Alan Greenspan (1997) gave a talk at Stanford in September 1997 with the title "Rules vs. Discretionary Monetary Policy," in which he discussed the Taylor rule and commented positively on the usefulness of monetary policy rules in general.

The same appears to be true internationally, which is a relevant consideration for this book. There was much mention of policy rules in the deliberations at other central banks around the world during the Great Moderation. I have used records of deliberations at the Norges Bank to assess the contagion of deviations from policy rules (the degree to which central banks follow each other) in recent years. I have also benefited from informal discussion with many central bankers in other countries over the years, and I have found that they are all familiar with policy rules and understand their value. I see no indication in these discussions that committee decision-making is incapable of handling discussions of a monetary policy strategy, or that such an approach eliminates the need for a strategy, though such a possibility was raised by Fischer (2017a).

An important research question is how discussions of policy rules evolved in more recent years at the FOMC, especially during the period in 2003–2005 when we saw more of a deviation from policy rules. To be sure, the records of the meetings and discussions may miss informal conversations and other key elements of any decision process at central banks, so some investigative reporting may be needed. Mallaby (2016) writes about the FOMC decision to keep interest rates low and to say that they would be low for a considerable period, and does not indicate one way or the other whether there was discussion that the rate was too low based on policy rules. Later, Bernanke (2010) argued that they were not too low based on policy rules if one used forecasts of inflation rather than actual inflation. As I pointed out in Taylor (2010), however, the Fed's forecasts were lower than actual inflation at the time, and the forecast wound up undershooting inflation over the forecast horizon.

Much of the policy changes in the 2009–2013 period were "balance sheet operations, as the Fed purchased Treasury securities and mortgage-backed securities on a large scale. I would classify these actions as discretionary rather than rule-like, in the sense I have used those terms in this book. The uncertainty and market disruption associated with the so-called taper tantrum in 2013 are illustrations of the dangers of too much discretion in balance sheet operations, and more recent Fed decisions seem to be steering clear of such actions.

Following this experience, the normalization process designed and described in the Fed's "Policy Normalization Principles and Plans" of September 2014 is consistent with a more rule-like approach, in which the FOMC "intends to reduce the Federal Reserve's securities holdings in a gradual and predictable manner." (p. 1) The "Addendum to the Policy Normalization Principles and Plans," issued in 2017, provides useful details about how the FOMC intends to reduce the Fed's securities holdings gradually by decreasing its reinvestment of principal payments.

Janet Yellen (2017a, 2017b), as the Fed chair, broke new ground in describing how monetary policy rules are used at the Fed. A follow-up presentation by Stanley Fischer (2017b), as the Fed vice-chair, and a new section of the June 2017 Monetary Policy Report continue in this vein.

Yellen (2017b, p. 2–3) summarized the Fed's strategy for the policy instruments as follows:

> When the economy is weak and unemployment is on the rise, we encourage spending and investing by pushing short-term interest rates lower. As you may know, the interest rate that we target is the federal funds rate, the rate banks charge each other for overnight loans. … Similarly, when the economy is threatening to push inflation too high down the road, we increase interest rates to keep the economy on a sustainable path and lean against its tendency to boom and then bust.

She then described "price stability" as a level of inflation of 2 percent a year, the maximum level of employment that can be sustained in the longer run as an unemployment rate of around 4.75 percent, and a "longer-run neutral rate" of the federal funds as a rate of 3 percent. One certainly could add more detail, but the statement includes the signs of the responses by the policy instruments, though not the magnitude. It mentions key factors driving the responses. And it gives numerical values for three key parameters. It could be usefully added to the Fed's *Statement on Longer-Run Goals and Monetary Policy Strategy*, which, despite its name, actually has no strategy for the instruments.

In a speech the following day, Yellen (2017a) provided charts and references to the specific policy rules. The purpose was to compare actual Fed policy with the Taylor rule and other rules and then to explain any differences. I think people found that useful, and it was good to see clarification of how the FOMC uses such policy rules in a constructive manner. An algebraic way to summarize the words in the presentations would be $r = p + ay + b(p-2) + 1$ with $a > 0$ and $b > 0$, where $r$ is the federal funds rate, $p$ is the rate of inflation, and

$y = 2.3(4.75 - u)$, where $u$ is the unemployment rate. (The 2.3 comes from Yellen, 2012.) In contrast, the Taylor rule is: $r = p + 0.5y + 0.5(p - 2) + 2$. This clearly provided context for a candid discussion. Fischer's (2017b) recent talk took a similar approach; he referred to decisions made in 2011 and more generally, explained how rules-based analysis feeds into the discussions and is evaluated by the FOMC to arrive at a policy decision.

The Fed's semiannual Monetary Policy Report (2017), issued on June 7, contained a whole new section called "Monetary Policy Rules and Their Role in the Federal Reserve's Policy Process." This section broke new ground. It listed three key principles of good monetary policy that the Fed said were being incorporated into policy rules; it then listed five policy rules, including the Taylor rule and four variations on that rule that the Fed used, with helpful references in notes.

The three principles sound quite reasonable: For one of them, sometimes called the "Taylor Principle," the Fed is quite specific, in that it gives the numerical range for the response of the policy rate–the federal funds rate–to the inflation rate.

More information, including some algebra, was given in the report. It is good that one of the five policy rules, which the Fed calls the "Taylor (1993) rule, adjusted," was based on the economic research of Reifschneider and Williams (2000), which I discussed earlier in this chapter. The Fed described these rules using the unemployment rate rather than real GDP, relying on Okun's Law, the empirical connection between the real GDP/potential GDP gap and the unemployment rate. One of the rules, what the Fed calls the "balanced-approach rule," is the Taylor rule with a different coefficient on the cyclical variable.

The report compared the FOMC's settings for the federal funds rate with the policy rules. It showed that the interest rate was too low for too long in the 2003–2005 period according to the Taylor rule, and that, according to three of the rules, the current federal funds rate should be moving up now. The Fed makes these calculations using its estimate of time-varying neutral rate of interest. However, aside from being positive about the three principles, it does not say much about its own policy strategy in the document.

The report focused on differences, rather than similarities, in the policy rules, and on the differences in inputs to the policy rules. The differences in measures of inflation, the equilibrium neutral interest rate, and other variables are part of monetary policymaking and always will be. They are a reason to use policy rules as a means of translating these differences in measurement into differences about policy in a systematic way. As I mentioned earlier in this chapter, such differences do not imply that policy rules or strategies are impractical.

In 2018, the Fed continued with this approach with a new chair, Jerome Powell. On February 23, the first Monetary Policy Report of the year again included a whole section on policy rules, elaborating on the July 2017 report, thus indicating that the new approach will continue.

Indeed, in his first congressional testimony before the Senate and the House of Representatives, Powell (2018, p. 4)) emphasized this view:

In evaluating the stance of monetary policy, the FOMC routinely consults monetary policy rules that connect prescriptions for the policy rate with variables associated with our mandated objectives. Personally, I find these rule prescriptions helpful. Careful judgments are required about the measurement of the variables used, as well as about the implications of the many issues these rules do not take into account. I would like to note that this Monetary Policy Report provides further discussion of monetary policy rules and their role in the Federal Reserve's policy process, extending the analysis we introduced in July.

This emphasis on rules and strategy did not go unnoticed by those who follow policy. As Larry Kudlow said just before he became director of the National Economic Council, "I've never seen that in any testimony before. … and I think that's progress." For more information, see Williams (2018). Later in the year, on March 8, the Fed posted a statement on its website on the principles and practices of sound monetary policy, with a very helpful note on "Policy Rules and How Policymakers Use Them."

The concept of policy rules is also affecting practical thinking on the international front. As discussed in the previous chapter, Paul Volcker (2014), Raghu Rajan (2016), and Mario Draghi all argued in favor of more transparent reaction functions. All are suggesting a more rule-based approach to the international monetary system.

## 2.5 How Does Proposed Legislation on Conducting Monetary Policy Fit into the Debate?

Several years ago, I discussed legislation that would require the Fed to establish and report on a policy rule for the interest rate or other instruments of policy (Taylor, 2011). The idea was based on economic research, including historical experience with prior legislative changes regarding the monetary aggregates. The legislation would not require that the Fed choose any specific rule, only that it establish some rule and report what the rule is. If the Fed deviated from its chosen strategy, the legislation would call on it to provide an explanation and answer questions at a public congressional hearing.

In Taylor (1993a), in which I discussed a simple policy rule as a guideline for monetary policy, I made no suggestion that the rule should be written into law, or even that it be used to monitor policy or hold central banks accountable. As I described in that paper, the objective was to help central bankers make their interest rate decisions in a less discretionary and more rule-like manner, and thereby achieve the goal of price stability and economic stability.

Why does legislation fit into the debate now? Because, as the debate reveals, there is evidence that, starting around 2003–2005, monetary policy became more discretionary and less rule-like than it was in the 1980s and 1990s. This history suggests that a legislated rule could help restore rule-like monetary principles and help prevent deviations in the future. It could also provide a catalyst for international monetary reform. In other words, the debate over such legislation fits directly into the debate about monetary policy rules versus discretion.

A proposal along these lines was written into legislative language in a bill that passed the House Financial Services Committee and the House of Representatives. The legislation is entitled "Requirements for Policy Rules of the Federal Open Market Committee," which is Section 2 of the Fed Oversight Reform and Modernization Act (FORM). This bill would require that the Fed "describe the strategy or rule of the Federal Open Market Committee for the systematic quantitative adjustment" of its policy instruments. It would be the Fed's job to choose the strategy and how to describe it. The Fed could change its strategy or deviate from it if circumstances called for a change, but it would have to explain why. The bill is still being debated, and it will likely be modified before passed into law as different views are expressed and discussed.

Precedent for this type of legislation appeared in sections of the Federal Reserve Act from 1977 to 2000, requiring the Fed to report the growth rate ranges of the monetary aggregates. The legislation did not specify exactly what the numerical settings of these ranges should be, but a greater focus on the money growth ranges was part of the disinflation efforts of the 1980s. When the requirement for reporting ranges for the monetary aggregates were removed from the law in 2000, nothing was put in its place.

A "Statement on Policy Rules Legislation" (Hansen et al., 2016) discusses reasons for the legislation, which would change how the Senate Banking Committee and the House Financial Services Committee oversee monetary policy. Allan Meltzer (2015) argued in congressional testimony, "We need change to improve the oversight that this Committee and the House Committee exercises over the Fed. You have the responsibility. Article I, Section 8 gives that to you. But you do not have the ability to exercise authority. You are busy people. You are involved in many issues. The Chairperson of the Fed is a person who has devoted his life to monetary policy. There is not any series of questions that you can ask on the fly that they are not going to be able to brush aside. So you need a rule which says, look, you said you were going to do this, and you have not done it. That requires an answer, and that I think is one of the most important reasons why we need some kind of a rule." (p. 6)

Janet Yellen (2015), as Fed chair, expressed concerns about the legislation, however. Testifying at the House Financial Services Committee, she said, "I don't believe that the Fed should chain itself to any mechanical rule." (p. 10) The legislation could be modified to address such concerns, and it is sensible to seek out compromises in which the Fed would choose, describe, and change its strategy, with no requirement that it be mechanical. The Fed would still serve as lender of last resort or take appropriate actions in the event of a crisis.

Some commentators say that the House monetary strategy bill would require the Fed to follow the Taylor rule, but this is not the case. The bill requires the Fed to describe how its strategy or rule might differ from a "reference rule," which happens to be the Taylor rule. While this could be modified, and compromises should be examined, describing the difference between specific policy rules and this reference rule is a natural and routine task for the Fed. In fact, many at the Fed already make such comparisons, including Yellen (2012, 2017a, 2017b).

Some argue that the zero bound on the interest rate means that policy rules are no longer useful. But as I described in this chapter, there are many ways for policy rules to deal with the ELB on the interest rate. Some argue that the decline in the equilibrium interest rate means that policy rules cannot be used. But one can easily adjust the equilibrium interest rate in the rule, as I also discussed in this chapter. Some argue that uncertainty about the output gap or the inflation rate renders useless rules that depend on the gap or the inflation rate. But that uncertainty is just as much a problem for discretion as it is for policy rules. Some argue that there are so many variants of policy rules, that you can't use rules in practice. It is true that some rules are better than others, and it makes perfect sense for researchers and policymakers to be looking for new and better rules. I think that research indicates the dangers of adding housing prices or the stock market to policy rules, but it is the job of the Fed to decide.

As I discussed previously, a possible problem with policy rules is that a monetary policy committee, such as the FOMC, might find it difficult to select a single rule when there are many differences of opinion on the committee about the rule. It might be particularly hard for the chair of the committee to forge a consensus. However, as with decisions about setting the policy interest rate, the possibility of dissent within the FOMC alleviates this problem because unanimity would not be required.

Finally, there are various ways to meet the requirements of the legislation. For example, rather than using a rule for the instruments of policy, the Fed might state a monetary strategy in terms of *inflation forecast targeting*, or simply *forecast targeting*. As I described earlier, according to this approach, the central bank would choose its policy interest rate so that a linear combination of its forecast of different variables would fall along a given path. While an interest rate path can be calculated, this approach does not yield a simple policy rule. According to the policy rules legislation, the central bank would have the job of deciding on the strategy. While experience suggests that focusing on the decision rule for monetary policy works better in practice, this alternative could possibly meet the terms of the proposed legislation.

## 2.6   Conclusion

Several takeaways emerge from this review of the debate over rules and discretion in monetary policy.

First, by and large, the different suggestions and proposals for policy rules over time have been based on specific economic models, robust methodologies, and empirical findings. That is an attractive feature of the policy evaluation, and it implies that high-quality economic research on monetary policy should be continued both inside and outside central banks.

The research has led to many policy rules for central bankers to choose among, and also to an understandable debate about the proposals and between the proposers. However, this is not a criticism, and this does not imply that central bankers should discard a systematic approach to policy. By analogy, in foreign policy, virtually all agree that it is crucial to have a strategy, so that policy is not all about tactics. But in any realistic situation, there are many proposed foreign policy strategies to choose among. It is the job of the policymaker to choose the strategy and make it work.

Second, while policy rules are often cast as ways to tie central bankers' hands, in reality, rules or strategies are simply ways to help central bankers improve monetary policy as they operate and communicate with markets and citizens in a democracy, and interact in a global monetary system. Experience over time in different countries shows that they do improve economic performance, and thereby improve people's lives.

Third, while quantitative, empirical, and historical methods are used in research to distinguish discretionary policy from rules-based policy, the line of demarcation is difficult to establish in practice. This makes comparing and contrasting the approaches difficult. Although important progress has been made, there is a need for further research. In the meantime, there are many ways that policymakers can internalize the principles of a clear and consistent strategy as they formulate their day-to-day decisions.

Fourth, research on policy rules has had a clear impact on the practice of central banking, even as the debate continues and enthusiasm for the ideas has waxed and waned. Detailed investigations based on transcripts and other documents show increasing impacts over time, as do informal conversations with policymakers. Research shows that this has occurred in central banks with varying degrees of committee decision-making. During the past year or so, there has been an increased focus on policy rules and strategies in speeches and commentaries by central bankers in the United States and other countries.

Fifth, while research shows that central bank independence is crucial for good monetary policymaking, it has not been enough to prevent swings away from rules-based policy. In the United States, where Congress has responsibility under the Constitution, this research suggests the value of considering legislation that would enhance reporting and discussions with Congress and the public about the strategy of monetary policy.

This chapter has addressed the key questions that define the scope of the recent debate between rules and discretion in monetary policy. The economic research described here shows why it is important that a rules-based reform of the international monetary system be based on an institutional reform in which a rules-based strategy is adopted at each central bank. There is a clear connection between the underlying economic theory and the proposed institutional reforms.

In the next chapter, I further explore this important connection between theory and institutions by tracing how monetary policy changed in response to changes in theory, and unfortunately, how it sometimes changes without a concomitant change in theory.

# 3 Do We Get More Out of Theory Than We Put In?

The question posed in the title to this chapter is timeless. Indeed, I used the same title a decade ago in a dinner talk at the Swiss National Bank (SNB). I got the idea for the title and the talk from a 1963 book, *The Feynman Lectures on Physics*, by the great physicist Richard Feynman. The book is a beautiful compendium of Feynman's introductory physics lectures at Cal Tech. As a teacher of introductory economics, I was particularly interested in what he had to say about teaching freshmen and sophomores.

Chapter 7, "The Theory of Gravitation," is particularly interesting. In it, Feynman wrote, "Any great discovery of a new law is useful only if we can take more out than we put in." He then went on to show that this was certainly true of the amazingly simple law of gravity. He showed how it predicted and explained many things not previously explained—such as the ebb and flow of tides and the roundness of the Earth—and how it was applied in many ways to improve people's lives.

In a similar vein, Mervyn King (2005), when he was governor of the Bank of England, said that he wished we could get more out of monetary theory, and I am sure that this is a frequent wish of all central bankers. It must surely be on the minds of researchers, whether in academia or in central banks, whether in monetary economics or other fields of endeavor. But wishing aside, do we get more out of monetary theory than we put in?

In this book, I have outlined a simple, fact-based theory of the workings of the international system. I showed why the world needs a policy reform of the system implied by that theory, and I explained how the reform should be implemented. Whether we get more out of that theory than we put in will depend on whether policy changes in accordance with the "why and how" of the theory, and on whether the theory is correct in its implication that such a reform will improve economic performance.

In this chapter, I take a real-time historical approach to the connection between theory, policy, and performance. I first recall where we were a decade ago by reviewing in the next section what I said when I spoke at the first annual Swiss National Bank Research Conference, using the talk as published in Taylor (2007a) as the benchmark. I then consider how things have changed in the past ten years.

## 3.1   The Way It Was a Decade Ago

Ten years ago, a heated debate was still going on in policy-making and academic circles about the role of monetary policy in bringing about the Great Moderation—the remarkable improvement in both price and output stability observed in the United States and other countries in the 1980s, 1990s, and through the early years of this century. Most notably, the frequency and severity of recessions declined sharply, along with the inflation rate.

My view back then was that monetary policy played an important role in achieving these good results. A key piece of evidence supporting this view was that a shift in the responsiveness of the monetary policy instruments occurred around the same time as the improvement in macroeconomic stability. Central banks, reflecting a greater focus on inflation, started systematically adjusting their policy interest rates in response to inflation by larger amounts and more quickly and systematically. Their responses to real gross domestic product (GDP) also changed. Hence, a Great Monetary Policy Shift accompanied the Great Moderation. This close timing provides strong evidence for a role for monetary policy in the improved economic performance.

What about the connection between monetary theory and this important shift in monetary policy? If indeed there is such a connection, then there is no doubt that we got a great deal more from theory than we put in. The timing suggests the strong possibility of a causal role for theory: Some thirty years earlier, monetary theorists set out to help improve the conduct of monetary policy, with the objective of making the fluctuations in real GDP and inflation smaller. They even wrote down that stability objective mathematically. And using a novel, expectations-based theory, they came up with new ideas for monetary policy, stressing the need for greater predictability and credibility, as well as larger responses of the instruments of policy to inflation and real GDP.

As we look back over the years before and during the Great Moderation, the shifts in the procedures for setting interest rates have been very close to what theory recommended, mainly in the systematic, prompt, and aggressive reactions of the policy interest rate to changes in inflation and real GDP. In parallel with those two changes, as I have already mentioned, the economy changed too: The fluctuations in inflation and real GDP came down, as was the objective of the theoretical research. This interaction between monetary theory, policy, and results is one of the most fascinating stories in economics. The connection between theory, policy, and results can never be proved beyond a shadow of a doubt, let alone the causal direction, but the timing is remarkably close.

### 3.1.1   The Three-Part Theory

To better access the causality from theory to policy, it is insightful to "look under the hood" and examine the engine of monetary theory. The main monetary theory during this period is well known to researchers in central banks. It has three parts, and in simple versions, this meant three equations, as in what is frequently called the New Keynesian model.

One part of this model describes price and wage adjustment; it describes how firms and workers set prices and wages and how these aggregate into the price level and the inflation rate. The second part of the model is the monetary policy rule, which describes how the central bank sets the policy rate. The third part of the model describes how the real economy is affected over time by the policy interest rate of the central bank; it is sometimes called the IS equation (for Investment and Saving) or the Euler equation, after the great Swiss mathematician Leonhard Euler who contributed much to the analysis of dynamic models.

While one could trace the influence of changes in all three parts of the model on monetary policy, most of the changes in theory in this period pertain to the first and second parts of the model, as the changes in the third part were relatively small. The second part—the monetary policy rule—was examined as part of the questions addressed in Chapter 2. In this chapter, I focus on changes in the first part of the model—the theory of price adjustment—and examine how these changes influenced policy.

### 3.1.2    Changes in Theory of Price Adjustment and Changes in Policy

The starting place for discussing the price adjustment model is the so-called expectations-augmented Phillips curve, which Milton Friedman and Edmund Phelps first suggested in the late 1960s. The expectations-augmented Phillips curve told us that if inflation rises above what people had expected, then output and employment will rise above normal levels, and vice versa. It also told us that if inflation is to be reduced below, or increased above, the level currently expected, then real output and employment have to fall below, or rise above, normal levels for a while. So long as expectations were assumed to be adaptive (i.e., to change slowly), this expectations-augmented Phillips curve gave a reasonably accurate description of the time series pattern of inflation and real GDP.

But with the advent of rational expectations, all this changed. If you assumed that expectations are rational and that prices are perfectly flexible, then monetary policy—so long as it is anticipated or followed a known rule—could not create a difference between the actual and expected inflation rates. There was no way for systematic monetary policy to affect real GDP. Only by surprising the public could the central bank affect real GDP. The central bank could achieve any inflation rate it wanted, with any degree of accuracy and with no adverse impact on the real economy.

Although this striking result attracted a lot of attention at the time, it was not a very accurate theory and was not useful for figuring out how monetary policy could reduce fluctuations in inflation and output. So a new theory was developed, one that endeavored to incorporate some real-world features of price and wage adjustment, along with rational expectations. The basic idea of the new theory is that firms would not change their prices instantaneously. (The same idea applies to wages, but I will focus on prices here.) Instead, there would be a period of time during which the firm's price would be fixed, and the pricing decisions of different firms would not all be made at the same time—price adjustments would be staggered and unsynchronized.

This new pricing assumption required a fundamental rethinking of the theory of markets. The typical textbook diagram of a demand curve, a supply curve, and an equilibrium price would not work. When you think about how a market might work in these circumstances, you realize that several important things are not included in the classic supply-and-demand framework. First, you realize that some firms' prices will be outstanding when another firm is deciding on a price to set. Thus, firms need to look back at the price decisions of others. Second, you realize that the firm's price will be around for a while, so it will have to think ahead and forecast the price decisions of other firms.

One way to get your hands around how such a market might work is to make a simplifying assumption that the price is set at a fixed level for a fixed period of time. In any case, this is what I assumed in my work on this problem in the 1970s (Taylor, 1979b, 1980). This simplifying assumption is akin to that of Paul Samuelson's original overlapping generation model that all people live for exactly two periods. Despite the simplicity of the assumption, the theory yields some fascinating results—and implications for policy. I will briefly outline these here.

First, the theory generates a simple equation that can be used in central bank models and tested. I list this as one of the seven key findings for the simple reason that had the theory not yielded this equation, none of the progress reported in this discussion would have been achieved. The equation describes the decision of firms setting prices today. A key variable in this equation is the prevailing price set by other firms, which is an average of prices set in the past and prices to be set in the future. There is a nice symmetry: the coefficients on the past and the future are equal.

The second key result is that expectations of future inflation matter for pricing decisions today. With the current price decision expected to last into the future, some prices set in the future will be relevant for today's decision. This is a very important result: For the first time, expectations of inflation come into play in the theory of inflation. It gives a rationale for central bank credibility and inflation targeting.

Third, there is inertia in the inflation process; and, therefore, past prices matter because they are relevant to present price decisions. The coefficients on past prices can be calculated from the theory.

Fourth, the inertia is longer than the length of the period during which prices are fixed. Price shocks take a long time to run through the market because the last period's price decisions depend on price decisions in the period before that, and so on into the distant past. This phenomenon is known as the *contract multiplier,* analogous to the Keynesian multiplier.

Fifth, the degree of inertia or persistence depends on monetary policy. The more aggressively the central bank responds to inflation, the less persistent inflation shocks are. This prediction was later shown to be true through practical experience and empirical analysis. Over time, inflation persistence came down as the monetary responses went up.

Sixth, the theory implies a trade-off curve between price stability and output stability. Inefficient monetary policies would be off the curve, and performance could be improved by moving on the curve. As discussed in Chapter 2, central bankers, including Federal Reserve (Fed) chair Ben Bernanke (2004), and later, governors of the Bank of England Mervyn King (2012) and Mark Carney (2013), used this curve to explain the role of monetary policy during the Great Moderation and other periods.

Seventh, the cost of disinflation is less than in the expectations-augmented Phillips curve. This prediction also proved accurate when people later examined the cost of disinflation of the early 1980s.

There were modifications to and extensions of the theory: Taylor (1979a) allowed for an empirical distribution of time intervals during which prices are fixed. Calvo (1982) assumed a geometric distribution, which led to further simplifications. Fuhrer and Moore (1995) modified the model so that it could generate additional inflation inertia, which was needed empirically. Fortunately, the policy implications remained robust to these changes. Later, the price adjustment equations were shown to be optimal if firms had some market power (see, for example, Yun, 1996; and Chari, Kehoe, and McGrattan, 2000).

Although the functional form of the optimization-based price-setting equation is the same as in the original model, we got even more out of this theory—an eighth result: More aggressive monetary policy responses imply a smaller pass-through of price shocks (commodities or exchange rates) to core inflation. Such a reduced pass-through has been documented in many countries. Other important recent developments were the addition of more flexibility in the timing of firms' price decisions (Dotsey, King, and Wolman, 1999; Gertler and Leahy, 2008; Golosov and Lucas, 2007) and sharper microeconomic tests of the theory (Klenow and Kryvtsov, 2008). The key policy results highlighted here continued to hold.

In summary, when I looked a decade ago at the theory of price adjustment, I saw strong policy implications and I realized that actual policy changed along the lines of those implications. If you add to this the finding that the change in policy played a role in achieving the dramatic and remarkable improvement in both price and output stability observed in the United States and other countries, then you come to the conclusion that we indeed got more out of that part of monetary theory than we put in. It was clear, of course, as I said then, that central bankers would face new practical problems in the future and that monetary research at central banks and elsewhere would need to focus on these practical problems if it is to continue to deliver. In any case, that's the way it was ten years ago.

## 3.2 The Way It Then Became

But an incipient change in policy was also underway, which would fundamentally change the history of the next ten years. A few weeks before the SNB conference, I gave a talk at the annual Kansas City Fed Conference held in Jackson Hole, Wyoming, where I showed that extra-low interest rates set by the Fed—a deviation from rule-based policy—were a factor in the housing boom (Taylor, 2007c). I illustrated this with two charts, reproduced here in figure 3.1. The chart in the upper panel of figure 3.1 shows the actual interest rate, the federal funds rate, set by the Fed over the period from 2000 to 2007. The upper chart also shows a counterfactual, rules-based interest rate in which the federal funds rate follows a Taylor rule, smoothed to have the 25-basis-point-increment adjustments commonly used by the Fed. As is clear from the chart, U.S. monetary policymakers departed significantly from the policy rule, especially in 2003–2005, by holding the

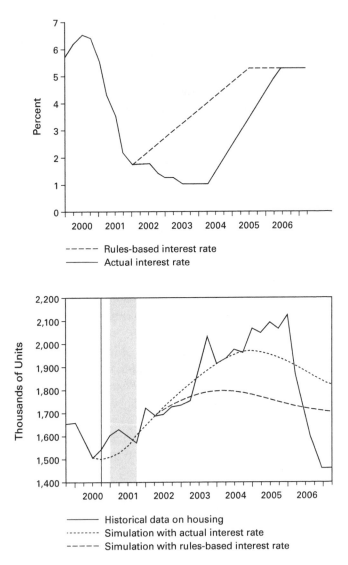

**Figure 3.1**
Actual and rules-based interest rate, along with housing starts: 2000–2006.
*Source*: Taylor (2007c).

federal funds rate below the interest rate setting that was implied by a policy rule.

I simulated a model of housing under these two interest rate paths for the federal funds rate. The model consisted of an equation in which housing starts depended on the federal funds rate, estimated with quarterly data over 50 years. The simulations are shown in the lower panel of figure 3.1, along with the actual historical data on housing starts. During the years from 2000 to 2002, when the policy is on the rule, the simulation tracks historical data on housing starts very closely. When the interest rate paths depart from each other starting in 2003, the housing boom continues according to the simulation with the actual interest rate set by the Fed, but not with counterfactual simulation of the higher rules-based interest rate. Hence, a rules-based interest rate path would have avoided much of the housing boom, according to this model, and thus the sharp bust associated with the Global Financial Crisis. The reversal of the boom, and thereby the resulting market turmoil, would not have been as sharp.

Although there was disagreement about this chart when I first presented it, the deviation of actual policy from the policy rule has been pointed out by many researchers over the past decade. Figure 3.2 shows a recently updated chart, produced by Boris Hofmann of the Bank for International Settlements (BIS). It includes a range of Taylor rates and its mean, and it continues through the end of 2017. (The range is computed as it was in figure 1.1 in chapter 1 for an average of central banks throughout the world and emerging markets.) The large deviation in 2003–2005 is still quite evident, as are the rules-based cut in interest rates in 2007–2009, the deviation after the Great Recession, and the beginning of normalization that occurred recently

The departure of policy in 2003–2005 compared with the policy of the 1990s also can be clearly seen without a policy

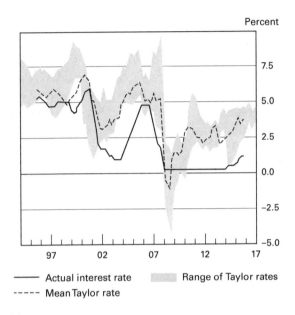

**Figure 3.2**
Actual interest rate and Taylor rule in the United States, 1995–2017. *Source:*
Boris Hofmann of the BIS.

rule. For example, in 1997, when the inflation rate was
2 percent, the interest rate was 5.5 percent. In 2003, with the
inflation rate also at 2 percent and the economy operating at
the same capacity level, the interest rate was only 1 percent.

Thus, there was a deviation in economic policy, followed
by a deterioration in economic performance. The departure
occurred before the Global Financial Crisis and clearly pre-
ceded the poor performance of recent years—evidence of
causality. A causal mechanism was that this departure
brought on a search for yield and excesses in the housing
market which, along with a regulatory process that departed
from rules for safety and soundness, helped bring on the

Global Financial Crisis. Thus, the predictions of the theory were borne out in practice again. There was clearly a move away from rule-like policy—defined by the Taylor rule or variants—and economic performance deteriorated.

And it was about that time that we were seeing other anomalies as well. I recall discussing with SNB policy-makers a decade ago in Zurich why the spread between the London Interbank Offered Rate (LIBOR) and the Overnight Index Swap (OIS) had widened, and whether this meant that there was a credit risk in the big banks. I started a research program with John Williams in response, in which we concluded (Taylor and Williams (2009)) that indeed the widened spread between LIBOR and OIS did indicate that there was an increase in counterparty risk between banks, and that the risk was related to concerns about securities derived from subprime mortgages and other assets. The Fed was originally quite critical of our research and did not accept the diagnosis. I advocated in Congress soon thereafter (Taylor, 2008) that as a first line of defense, central banks should reduce their policy interest rate by the increased spread between LIBOR and OIS, which was about 50 basis points at the time, and then find out about the credit risk. I was effectively suggesting that the Fed use the SNB operating procedure of that time.

When the panic struck in the fall of 2008, the Fed and many other central banks responded very well, acting as traditional lenders of last resort. But soon the departures from rule-like monetary policy returned, especially if you include the discretionary and massive quantitative easing, the use of frequently changing forward guidance, and the talk about discretionary macroprudential policy. Recall that Nikolsko-Rzhevskyy, Papell, and Prodan (2014), using interest rate rules as a measure of rules-based policies, showed that there was a deviation, and that deviation had harmful effects on the economy.

The fact that the deviation was global was first pointed out by Ahrend (2010) at the Organisation for Economic Co-operation and Development (OECD), and this is now obvious to any observer, as figure 1.1 makes clear. Central banks followed each other down with extra-low interest rates or the use of quantitative easing. Richard Clarida (2016) remarked that "QE begets QE!" Complaints about spillover were heard more and more often, and pleas for some international coordination grew. Economists began to call for a return to rules-based policy.

Michael Belongia and Peter Ireland (2015) said: "For all the talk about 'transparency,' ... the process—or rule—by which the [Federal Open Market Committee (FOMC)] intends to defend its two-percent inflation target remains unknown." Charles Calomiris, Mickey Levy, and Peter Ireland (2015) wrote that rules-based monetary policy made even more sense than decades before, remarking in particular that "the Taylor Rule appears, if anything, to be even better suited to guiding Fed policy today." (p. 7) Why did they conclude this? They noted that while the target inflation rate of 2 percent was assumed in that rule, the Fed set the value at 2 percent, and thus the "Taylor Rule is designed quite specifically to bring about precisely the type of price stability that the FOMC has promised." (p. 7) What's more, they noted that 25 years ago, "few economists would have guessed that outright deflation would become the biggest perceived threat to central bankers around the world, yet the Taylor Rule not only anticipates this, its ingenious design tackles the problem head on ... the Taylor Rule is therefore fully consistent with the Federal Reserve's statutory dual mandate" (p. 7–8).

### 3.2.1   Was There a Change in Theory?

What has been most striking about this past decade is that this change in monetary policy was not accompanied by a change in monetary theory, at least not in the theory of price adjustment that is the focus of this chapter. In a contribution to *The Handbook of Macroeconomics*, I wrote about "The Staying Power of Staggered Wage and Price Setting Models in Macroeconomics" (Taylor, 2016c). I showed that the data behind this theory had grown exponentially over time and across countries, and that there was a greater need for heterogeneity in the models. But I also concluded that the same basic policy implications remained, much as I had summarized ten years earlier and have reviewed here. And these same ideas continued to be embedded in monetary models used both inside and outside of central banks.

In looking back at the past decade, therefore, one must conclude that we did *not* get more out of theory than we put in. The reason for this is not that the theory went wrong, but rather that the policy went off track. To get more out of theory than we put in, we need to use the theory, and the change in policy suggests that the theory was not used. Although economics is nowhere near as precise as physics, it is as if people started building and flying airplanes while ignoring the theory of gravity.

### 3.3   Which Way Will It Be in the Future?

We are at another turning point now, with respect to both the international monetary system and the monetary policy of each country that forms the system. I have argued that monetary theory—as updated with recent data and experience—suggests a policy reform that will result in a rules-based international monetary system. The starting point is a return to a rules-based system in each country.

I think that we will get more out of this theory than we put in, but, as the history makes clear, this will require that the reforms actually occur. It is very promising that central bankers throughout the world are talking about normalization. It is good that the Fed has begun to bring new focus to rules-based policy. But there are many different views about monetary policy, and there is a risk that policy will not move in that direction.

Another risk is that there will be a change in monetary theory that will turn out to be misleading. Economic research is exciting, as are the pursuit and development of new theories; this is how progress has been and will be made. But perhaps there will be a detour—a new theory that becomes popular and seems to suggest that rules-based policy does not work, but that is actually incorrect, and later proved wrong. This would lead us away from—or at least delay the renewal of—rules-based policy, and thus perpetuate the deviation from good policy and a subsequent deterioration in performance. Awareness of such risks at central banks and in the community of economic researchers will reduce the likelihood of their being realized.

# Notes

1. As explained by the BIS, "The Taylor rates are calculated as $i = r^* + \pi^* + 1.5(\pi - \pi^*) + 0.5y$, where $\pi$ is a measure of inflation, $y$ is a measure of the output gap, $\pi^*$ is the inflation target, and $r^*$ is the long-run real interest rate, here proxied by real trend output growth. The graph shows the mean and the range of the Taylor rates of different inflation/output gap combinations, obtained by combining four measures of inflation (headline, core, GDP deflator, and consensus headline forecasts) with four measures of the output gap (obtained using Hodrick-Prescott (HP) filter, segmented linear trend and unobserved components techniques, and IMF estimates). $\pi^*$ is set equal to the official inflation target/objective, and otherwise to the sample average or trend inflation estimated through a standard HP filter." See Hofmann and Bogdanova (2012) for more detail.

2. The information was drawn from several monetary policy reports of the Norges Bank and was used in a presentation that I made at the Norges Bank in 2010, later published in Taylor (2013).

3. The multiplier is $1/(1-\alpha\alpha^*)$, where $\alpha$ is the reaction of one central bank and $\alpha^*$ is the reaction of the other central bank. For the case in Figure 2, $\alpha = 0.5$ and $\alpha^* = 1$, so the multiplier is 2.

4. If the increase in reserve balances was used to buy foreign bonds, it would not be a so-called sterilized intervention because the central bank would not be selling domestic bonds to offset the purchase of foreign bonds.

5. The 2003–2005 episode is discussed further in chapter 3.

6. *Journal of Policy Modeling*, vol. 36, no. 4, 2013.

# References

Ahrend, Rudiger. (2010). "Monetary Ease: A Factor behind Financial Crises? Some Evidence from OECD Countries." *Economics: The Open Access, Open Assessment E-Journal*, vol. 4, no. 2010–2012, April 14. http://www.economics -ejournal.org/economics/journalarticles/2010-12.

Anderson, Theodore W., and John B. Taylor. (1976). "Some Experimental Results on the Statistical Properties of Least Squares Estimates in Control Problems." *Econometrica*, vol. 44, no. 6, 1289–1302.

Ando, Albert, and Robert Rasche. (1971). "Equations in the MIT-PENN-SSRC Econometric Model of the United States." Unpublished paper. January, University of Pennsylvania.

Asso, Pier Francesco, and Robert Leeson. (2012). "Monetary Policy Rules: From Adam Smith to John Taylor," in *The Taylor Rule and the Transformation of Monetary Policy*, Evan F. Koenig, Robert Leeson, and George A. Kahn, eds. Stanford, CA: Hoover Institution Press, pp. 3–62.

Beckworth, D., and J. R. Hendrickson. (2015). *Nominal GDP Targeting and the Taylor Rule on an Even Playing Field*. Working paper, Western Kentucky University, Department of Economics, Bowling Green.

Belongia, Michael, and Peter Ireland. (2014). "Interest Rates and Money in the Measurement of Monetary Policy," NBER Working Paper No. 20134, May. Cambridge, MA: National Bureau of Economic Research (NBER).

Belongia, Michael, and Peter Ireland. (2015). "Don't Audit the Fed, Restructure It," *e21*, February 19. https://economics21.org/html/don%E2%80%99t -audit-fed-restructure-it-1249.html.

Bernanke, Ben. (2003). "Remarks Before the Money Marketeers of New York University," New York, February 3. https://www.federalreserve.gov/board docs/speeches/2003/20030203/default.htm.

Bernanke, Ben. (2004). "The Great Moderation." Eastern Economic Association, February 20, Washington, DC. https://www.federalreserve.gov/board docs/speeches/2004/20040220/.

Bernanke, Ben S. (2010). "Monetary Policy and the Housing Bubble." Annual Meeting of the American Economic Association, Atlanta, GA, January 3. https://www.federalreserve.gov/newsevents/speech/bernanke20100103a .htm.

Bernanke, Ben. (2015). *Objections to Federal Reserve Accountability Bill.* Video of remarks at the Conference on The Fed in the 21st Century: Independence, Governance, and Accountability, Brookings Institution, Washington, DC, March 2. https://www.youtube.com/watch?v=KJmA5JDNpKg&t=37.

Board of Governors of the Federal Reserve System. (2017). *Monetary Policy Report,* June 7.

Board of Governors of the Federal Reserve System. (2018). *Monetary Policy Report,* February 23.

Bordo, Michael D., and Andrew T. Levin. (2017). "Central Bank Digital Currency and the Future of Monetary Policy," in *The Structural Foundations of Monetary Policy,* Michael Bordo, John Cochrane, and Amit Seru, eds. Stanford, CA: Hoover Institution Press, pp. 143–178.

Brayton, Flint, Andrew Levin, Ralph Tryon, and John C. Williams. (1997). "The Evolution of Macro Models at the Federal Reserve Board," *Carnegie-Rochester Conference Series on Public Policy,* vol. 47, 43–81.

Brayton, Flint, Peter Tinsley, A. Bomfim, D. Reifschneider, P. von zur Muehlen, B. Tetlow, and J. Williams. (1996). *A Guide to FRB/US: A Macroeconomic Model of the United States.* Washington, DC: Federal Reserve Board. https://www.federalreserve.gov/pubs/feds/1996/199642/199642pap .pdf.

Brunner, Karl. (1968). "The Role of Money and Monetary Policy." July 1968 Federal Reserve Bank of St Louis *Review,* pp. 9–24.

Brunner, Karl. (1971). "A Survey of Selected Issues in Monetary Theory," *Schweizerische Zeitschrift für Volkswirtschaft und Statistik,* no. 1, Jhargang 107, March, pp. 1–46.

Brunner, Karl. (1980). "The Control of Monetary Aggregates." In *Controlling Monetary Aggregates III* (pp. 1–65). Boston: Federal Reserve Bank of Boston.

Brunner, Karl and Allan Meltzer (1976). "Introduction to the Series," *Carnegie-Rochester Conference Series on Public Policy*, Elsevier, vol. 1, p ii.

Brunner, Karl and Allan Meltzer. (1993). *Money and the Economy: Issues in Monetary Analysis*, Cambridge University Press.

Bryant, Ralph, Peter Hooper, and Catherine Mann. (1993). *Evaluating Policy Regimes: New Research in Empirical Macroeconomics.* Washington, DC: Brookings Institution.

Calomiris, Charles, Peter Ireland, and Mickey Levy. (2015). "Guidelines for Policymaking and Communications during Normalization." Shadow Open Market Committee, March 20. http://shadowfed.org/wp-content/uploads /2015/03/CalomirisIrelandLevySOMC-March2015.pdf.

Calvo, Guillermo. (1982). "Staggered Contracts and Exchange Rate Policy," in *Exchange Rates and International Macroeconomics*, J. A. Frankel, ed. Chicago: University of Chicago Press, pp. 235–258.

Carney, Mark. (2013). "Monetary Policy after the Fall." Eric J. Hanson Memorial Lecture, University of Alberta, Edmonton, Alberta, May 1, https://www .bankofcanada.ca/wp-content/uploads/2013/05/remarks-010513.pdf.

Carstens, Agustin. (2015). "Challenges for Emerging Economies in the Face of Unconventional Monetary Policies in Advanced Economies." Stavros Niarchos Foundation Lecture, Peterson Institute for International Economics, Washington, DC, April 20.

Carstens, Agustin. (2016). "Overview Panel: The Case for Emerging Market Economies." In *Designing Resilient Monetary Policy Frameworks for the Future.* Kansas City: Federal Reserve Bank of Kansas City, pp. 501–509.

Chari, V. V., Patrick Kehoe, and Ellen McGrattan. (2000). "Sticky Price Models of the Business Cycle: Can the Contract Multiplier Solve the Persistence Problem?" *Econometrica*, vol. 68, 1151–1179.

Chen, Qianying, Andrew Filardo, Dong He, and Feng Zhu. (2012). "International Spillovers of Central Bank Balance Sheet Policies," BIS Papers, Number 66. Basel, Switzerland: Bank for International Settlements (BIS).

Clarida, Richard. (2016). "Comments on John B. Taylor, 'The Federal Reserve in a Globalized World Economy,'" in *The Federal Reserve's Role in the Globalized World Economy: A Historical Perspective*, Michael Bordo and Mark A. Wynne, eds. New York: Cambridge University Press, pp. 218–219.

Clarida, Richard, Jordi Gali, and Mark Gertler. (2000). "Monetary Policy Rules and Macroeconomic Stability: Evidence and Some Theory." *Quarterly Journal of Economics*, vol. 115, no. 1, 147–180.

Coeuré, Benoît. (2017). "The International Dimension of the ECB's Asset Purchase Programme." Speech at the Foreign Exchange Contact Group Meeting, July 11, Frankfurt, Germany.

Coletti, Donald, Benjamin Hunt, David Rose, and Robert Tetlow. (1996). "The Bank of Canada's New Quarterly Projection Model: Part 3: The Dynamic Model," Bank of Canada, Technical Report, no. 75, May.

Cukierman, Alex. (2017). "Forex Intervention and Reserve Management in Switzerland and Israel since the Financial Crisis: Comparison and Policy Lessons." Interdisciplinary Center, Tel-Aviv University. https://gdre-scpo-aix .sciencesconf.org/195876/document.

de Leeuw, Frank, and Edward Gramlich. (1968). "The Federal Reserve–MIT Econometric Model." *Federal Reserve Bulletin*, vol. 54, 11–40.

Dellas, Harris, and George S. Tavlas. (2017). "Milton Friedman and the Case for Flexible Exchange Rates and Monetary Rules," Working Paper 236. Athens: Bank of Greece. https://www.bankofgreece.gr/BogEkdoseis/Paper 2017236.pdf.

Dorn, James A. (2018). "Monetary Policy in an Uncertain World: The Case for Rules," *The Cato Journal*, vol. 38, no. 1.

Dotsey, Michael. (2016). "Comment on Alex Nikolsko-Rzhevskyy, David H. Papell, and Ruxandra Prodan 'Policy Rule Legislation in Practice,'" in *Central Bank Governance and Oversight Reform*, John H. Cochrane and John B. Taylor, eds. Stanford, CA: Hoover Institution Press.

Dotsey, Michael, Robert King, and Alex Wolman. (1999). "State Dependent Pricing and the General Equilibrium Dynamics of Money and Output." *Quarterly Journal of Economics*, vol. 114, 655–690.

Draghi, Mario. (2016). "The International Dimension of Monetary Policy," The ECB Forum on Central Banking, Sintra, Portugal, June 28. https://www .ecb.europa.eu/press/key/date/2016/html/sp160628.en.html

Edwards, Sebastian. (2017). "Monetary Policy Independence under Flexible Exchange Rates: The Federal Reserve and Monetary Policy in Latin America—Is There Policy Spillover?" in *Rules for International Monetary Stability*, Michael Bordo and John B. Taylor, eds. Stanford, CA: Hoover Institution Press, pp. 1–47.

Eichengreen, Barry. (2004). *Capital Flows and Crises*. Cambridge, MA: MIT Press, p. 307n1.

Engel, Charles, and Kenneth West. (2006). "Taylor Rules and the Deutsche-Dollar Real Exchange Rate," *Journal of Money Credit and Banking*, vol. 38, 1175–1194.

Fagan, G., J. R. Lothian, and P. D. McNelis. (2013). "Was the Gold Standard Really Destabilizing?" *Journal of Applied Econometrics*, vol. 8, 131–249.

Fair, Ray, and John B. Taylor. (1983). "Solution and Maximum Likelihood Estimation of Dynamic Nonlinear Rational Expectations Models." *Econometrica*, vol. 51, no. 4, 1169–1185.

Feynman, Richard. (1963). *The Feynman Lectures on Physics*. Available online as Richard Feynman, Robert Leighton, and Matthew Sands, http://www.feynmanlectures.caltech.edu.

Filardo, Andrew, and James Yetman. (2012). "The Expansion of Central Bank Balance Sheets in Emerging Asia: What Are the Risks?" *BIS Quarterly Review*, June. https://www.bis.org/publ/qtrpdf/r_qt1206g.pdf.

Fischer, Stanley. (2017a). "Committee Decisions and Monetary Policy Rules," in *The Structural Foundations of Monetary Policy*, Michael Bordo, John Cochrane, and Amit Seru, eds. Stanford, CA: Hoover Institution Press, pp. 201–211.

Fischer, Stanley. (2017b). "I'd Rather Have Bob Solow than an Econometric Model, But …" Speech at the Warwick Economics Summit, Coventry, United Kingdom. February, https://www.federalreserve.gov/newsevents/speech/fischer20170211a.htm.

Fisher, Irving. (1920). *Stabilizing the Dollar.* New York: Macmillan.

FOMC—Federal Open Market Committee. (2014). "Policy Normalization Principles and Plans," as adopted effective September 16.

FOMC—Federal Open Market Committee. (2017). "Addendum to the Policy Normalization Principles and Plans," as adopted effective June 1.

Friedman, Milton. (1948). "A Monetary and Fiscal Framework for Economic Stability." *American Economic Review*, vol. 38, no. 3, 245–264.

Friedman, Milton. (1953). "The Case for Flexible Exchange Rates," *Essays in Positive Economics*. Chicago: University of Chicago Press, pp. 157–203.

Fuhrer, Jeffrey, and George Moore. (1995). "Inflation Persistence." *Quarterly Journal of Economics*, vol. 110, 127–159.

Gawande, Atul. (2007). "The Checklist: If Something So Simple Can Transform Intensive Care, What Else Can It Do?" *The New Yorker*, December 19. http://www.newyorker.com/magazine/2007/12/10/the-checklist.

Gertler, Mark, and John Leahy. (2008). "A Phillips Curve with an (S,s) Foundation," *Journal of Political Economy*, vol. 116, no. 3, 533–572.

Ghosh, Atish, Jonathan Ostry, and Mahvash Qureshi. (2017). *Taming the Tide of Capital Flows: A Policy Guide.* Cambridge, MA: MIT Press.

Giannoni, Marc P., and Michael Woodford. (2005). "Optimal Inflation Targeting Rules," in *The Inflation-Targeting Debate*, Ben S. Bernanke and Michael Woodford, eds., National Bureau of Economic Research (NBER), University of Chicago Press, Chicago, pp. 93–172

Golosov, Michael, and Robert Lucas, Jr. (2007). "Menu Costs and the Phillips Curve." *Journal of Political Economy*, vol. 115, no. 2, 171–199.

Gray, Colin. (2013). "Responding to a Monetary Superpower: Investigating the Behavioral Spillovers of U.S. Monetary Policy." *Atlantic Economic Journal*, vol. 21, no. 2, 173–184.

Greenspan, Alan (1997). "Rules vs. discretionary monetary policy," Remarks at the 15th Anniversary Conference of the Center for Economic Policy Research at Stanford University, Stanford, California, September 5, https://www.federalreserve.gov/boarddocs/speeches/1997/19970905.htm.

Hansen, Lars Peter, Robert Lucas, Edward Prescott, et al. (2016). "Statement on Policy Rules Legislation." https://web.stanford.edu/~johntayl/2016_pdfs/Statement_on_Policy_Rules_Legislation_2-29-2016.pdf.

He, Dong, and Robert N. McCauley. (2013). "Transmitting Global Liquidity to East Asia: Policy Rates, Bond Yields, Currencies, and Dollar Credit," BIS Working Paper No. 431. Basel, Switzerland: Bank of International Settlements (BIS).

Helliwell, John, Lawrence Officer, Harold Shapiro, and Ian Stewart. (1969). "The Structure of RDX1." Bank of Canada Staff Research Study, no. 3.

Hetzel, Robert. (1987). "Henry Thornton: Seminal Monetary Theorist and Father of the Modern Central Bank." *Economic Review*, Federal Reserve Bank of Richmond, July/August, 3–16. https://www.richmondfed.org/-/media/richmondfedorg/publications/research/economic_review/1987/pdf/er730401.pdf.

Hofmann, B., and B. Bogdanova. (2012). "Taylor Rules and Monetary Policy: A Global 'Great Deviation'?" *BIS Quarterly Review*, September, 37–49.

Holston, Kathryn, Thomas Laubach, and John C. Williams. (2016). "Measuring the Natural Rate of Interest: International Trends and Determinants," Federal Reserve Bank of San Francisco Working Paper 2016-11. http://www.frbsf.org/economic-research/publications/workingpapers/wp2016-11.pdf.

IMF Staff Report. (2015). "Monetary Policy and Financial Stability," International Monetary Fund, Washington, DC, August 28.

Kahn, George A. (2010). "Taylor Rule Deviations and Financial Imbalances." *Economic Review*, Federal Reserve Bank of Kansas City, Second Quarter, 63–99.

Kahn, George A. (2012). "The Taylor Rule and the Practice of Central Banking," in *The Taylor Rule and the Transformation of Monetary Policy*, Evan F. Koenig, Robert Leeson, and George A. Kahn, eds. Hoover Institution Press, pp. 63–101

King, Mervyn. (2003). "Speech at the East Midlands Development Agency/Bank of England Dinner," Leicester, United Kingdom, October 14.

King, Mervyn. (2005). "Monetary Policy: Practice Ahead of Theory," Mais Lecture, Cass Business School, City University, London, May 17

King, Mervyn. (2012). "Twenty Years of Inflation Targeting," Stamp Memorial Lecture, London School of Economics, London, October 9.

Klenow, Peter, and Oleksiy Kryvtsov. (2008). "State Dependent or Time Dependent Pricing: Does It Matter for Recent U.S. Inflation?" *Quarterly Journal of Economics*, vol. 73, no. 3, 863–904.

Kohn, Donald. (2012). "It's Not So Simple," in *The Taylor Rule and the Transformation of Monetary Policy*, Evan F. Koenig, Robert Leeson, and George A. Kahn, eds Stanford, CA: Hoover Institution Press, pp. 173–182

Kydland, Finn, and Edward Prescott. (1977). "Rules Rather than Discretion: The Inconsistency of Optimal Plans." *Journal of Political Economy vol. 85, no. 3*, 618–637.

Lane, Timothy. (2016). "Monetary Policy and Financial Stability—Looking for the Right Tools," Bank of Canada, February 8. https://www.bankofcanada.ca/wp-content/uploads/2016/02/remarks-080216.pdf

Laubach, Thomas, and John C. Williams. (2003). "Measuring the Natural Rate of Interest." *Review of Economics and Statistics*, vol. 85, no. 4, 1063–1070.

Laubach, Thomas, and John C. Williams. (2016). "Measuring the Natural Rate of Interest Redux." *Business Economics*, vol. 51, 257–267.

Levin, Andrew T., and John C. Williams. (2003). "Robust Monetary Policy with Competing Reference Models." *Journal of Monetary Economics*, vol. 50, 945–975.

Lipsky, John. (2012). "A View from the Financial Markets," in *The Taylor Rule and the Transformation of Monetary Policy*, Evan F. Koenig, Robert Leeson, and George A. Kahn, eds. Stanford, CA: Hoover Institution Press.

Lombra, Raymond E., and Michael Moran. (1980). "Policy Advice and Policymaking at the Federal Reserve." *Journal of Monetary Economics*, Fall, 9–68.

Lucas, Robert E. (1976). "Econometric Policy Evaluation: A Critique." *Carnegie-Rochester Conference Series on Public Policy*, vol. 1, 19–46.

Maliar, Lilia, Serguei Maliar, John B. Taylor, and Inna Tsener. (2015). "A Tractable Framework for Analyzing a Class of Nonstationary Markov Models," NBER Working Paper 21155. Cambridge, MA: National Bureau of Economic Research.

Mallaby, Sebastian. (2016). *The Man Who Knew*. New York: Penguin.

McCallum, Bennett. (1999). "Issues in the Design of Monetary Policy Rules." In *Handbook of Macroeconomics*, John B. Taylor and Michael Woodford, eds. Amsterdam: Elsevier, pp. 1483–1530.

Meltzer, Allan H. (1992). "Karl Brunner: In Memoriam." *The Cato Journal*, vol. 12, no. 1, 1–5.

Meltzer, Allan H. (2015). "Karl Brunner, Scholar: An Appreciation." Hoover Institution Economics Working Paper WP15116, December, Stanford University

Meltzer, Allan. (2012). "Federal Reserve Policy in the Great Recession." *Cato Journal*, vol. 32, no. 2, 255–263.

Meltzer, Allan. (2015). Transcript, Hearing Before the Committee on Banking, Housing, and Urban Affairs, U.S. Senate, March 3. https://www.gpo.gov/fdsys/pkg/CHRG-114shrg93893/html/CHRG-114shrg93893.htm.

Meltzer, Allan H. (2016). "Remarks," in "General Discussion: Funding Quantitative Easing to Target Inflation," in *Designing Resilient Monetary Policy Frameworks for the Future*, Federal Reserve Bank of Kansas City, 493–500.

Morgenthau, Henry. (1944). "Closing Address to the Conference," United Nations Monetary and Financial Conference, Bretton Woods, New Hampshire, July.

Newey, Whitney, and Kenneth West. (1987). "A Simple, Positive Semi-definite, Heteroskedasticity and Autocorrelation Consistent Covariance Matrix." *Econometrica*, vol. 55, no. 3, 703–708.

Nikolsko-Rzhevskyy, Alex, David H. Papell, and Ruxandra Prodan. (2014). "Deviations from Rules-Based Policy and Their Effects," in *Frameworks for Central Banking in the Next Century*, Michael D. Bordo, William Dupor, and John B. Taylor (eds.), A Special Issue on the Occasion of the Centennial of the Founding of the Federal Reserve. *Journal of Economics Dynamics and Control*, vol. 49, 4–17.

Nurkse, Ragnar. (1944). *International Currency Experience*. Geneva, Switzerland: League of Nations, pp. 117–122.

Orphanides, A. (2003). "Monetary Policy Evaluation with Noisy Information." *Journal of Monetary Economics*, vol. 50, no. 3, 605–631.

Orphanides, Athanasios, and John C. Williams. (2008). "Learning, Expectations Formation, and the Pitfalls of Optimal Control Monetary Policy." *Journal of Monetary Economics*, vol. 55S, S80–S96.

Phillips, A. W. (1954). "Stabilization Policy in a Closed Economy." *Economic Journal*, vol. 64, 290–323.

Poloz, Stephen, David Rose, and Robert Tetlow. (1994). "The Bank of Canada's New Quarterly Projection Model (QPM): An Introduction." *Bank of Canada Review*, Autumn, 23–38.

Powell, Jerome H. (2018). "Semiannual Monetary Policy Report to the Congress." Testimony Before the Committee on Financial Services, U.S. House of Representatives, Washington, DC, February 27, 2018.

Qvigstad, Jan F. (2005). "When Does an Interest Rate Path `Look Good'? Criteria for an Appropriate Future Interest Rate Path—A Practitioner's Approach." Norges Bank Staff Memo: Monetary Policy, No. 2005/6, June 15, Oslo.

Rajan, Raghuram. (2016). "New Rules for the Monetary Game." *Project Syndicate*, March 2.

Ramey, Valerie. (2016). "Macroeconomic Shocks and Their Propagation, in *Handbook of Macroeconomics, Vol. 2*, John B. Taylor and Harald Uhlig, eds. Amsterdam: Elsevier Science, pp. 71–162.

Reifschneider, David, and John C. Williams. (2000). "Three Lessons for Monetary Policy in a Low Inflation Era." *Journal of Money, Credit, and Banking*, vol. 32, no. 4, 936–966.

Rey, Helene. (2013). "Dilemma not Trilemma: The Global Financial Cycle and Monetary Policy Independence," in *Global Dimensions of Unconventional Monetary Policy*, Jackson Hole Conference, Federal Reserve Bank of Kansas City, pp. 285–333.

Ricardo, David. (1824). *Plan for the Establishment of a National Bank*. Reprinted in David Ricardo (1951), *The Works and Correspondence of David Ricardo*.

*Volume 4: Pamphlets and Papers 1815–1823.* Cambridge: Cambridge University Press.

Shin, Hyun Song. (2017). "Monetary Policy Challenges Posed by Global Liquidity." High-Level Roundtable on Central Banking in Asia, 50th ADB Annual Meeting, Yokohama, Japan, May 6, 2017.

Shultz, George. (2014). "The Importance of Rules-Based Policy in Practice," in *Frameworks for Central Banking in the Next Century*, Michael D. Bordo, William Dupor, and John B. Taylor, eds. *Journal of Economic Dynamics and Control*, vol. 49, December, 142–143

Simons, Henry. (1936). "Rules Versus Authorities in Monetary Policy." *Journal of Political Economy*, vol. 44, no. 1, 1–30.

Skolimowski, Piotr. (2017). "This Magic Formula Reveals How the ECB Might Taper," *Bloomberg News*, July 16. https://www.bloomberg.com /news/articles/2017-07-17/this-magic-formula-reveals-how-the-ecb-might -taper.

Smith, Adam. (1776). *An Inquiry into the Nature and Causes of the Wealth of Nations.* London: Methuen and Co.

Summers, Lawrence. (2014). "Remarks in Discussion on Session 1: 'Growth or Stagnation for the US Economy,'" *Journal of Policy Modeling*, vol. 36, no. 4, 697.

Sumner, Scott. (2014). "Nominal GDP Targeting: A Simple Rule to Improve Fed Performance." *Cato Journal*, vol. 34, no. 2, 315–337.

Svensson, Lars E. O. (1998). "Inflation Forecast Targeting: Implementing and Monitoring Inflation Targets." *European Economic Review*, 41, 1111–1146.

Taylor, John B. (1979a). "An Econometric Business Cycle Model with Rational Expectations," Columbia University Working Paper. New York: Columbia University.

Taylor, John B. (1979b). "Estimation and Control of a Macroeconomic Model with Rational Expectations." *Econometrica*, vol. 47, no. 5, 1267–1286.

Taylor, John B. (1980). "Aggregate Dynamics and Staggered Contracts," *Journal of Political Economy*, vol. 88, 1–23.

Taylor, John B. (1985). "International Coordination in the Design of Macroeconomic Policy Rules." *European Economic Review*, vol. 28, 53–81.

Taylor, John B. (1988). "The Treatment of Expectations in Large Multicountry Models," in *Empirical Macroeconomics for Interdependent Economies,*

Ralph Bryant et al., eds. Washington, DC, The Brookings Institution, pp. 161–182.

Taylor, John B. (1993a). "Discretion Versus Policy Rules in Practice." *Carnegie-Rochester Series on Public Policy*, 39, 195–214.

Taylor, John B. (1993b). *Macroeconomic Policy in a World Economy: From Econometric Design to Practical Operation*. New York: W. W. Norton. https://web .stanford.edu/~johntayl/MacroPolicyWorld.htm.

Taylor, John B. (1993c). Part of "Invited Contributors: Selected Comments and Reflections," in *Evaluating Policy Regimes: New Research in Empirical Macroeconomics*, Ralph Bryant, Peter Hooper, and Catherine Mann. (1993). Washington, DC: Brookings Institution, p. 426.

Taylor, John B. (1996). "Policy Rules as a Means to a More Effective Monetary Policy." *Monetary and Economic Studies*, vol. 14, no. 1, 28–39.

Taylor, John B. (1998a). "Applying Academic Research on Monetary Policy Rules: An Exercise in Translational Economics." The Harry G. Johnson Lecture. *The Manchester School Supplement*, vol. 66, 1–16.

Taylor, John B. (1998b). "Monetary Policy and the Long Boom," *Federal Reserve Bank of St. Louis Review*, November/December, 3–11.

Taylor, John B. (2001). "Expectations, Open Market Operations, and Changes in the Federal Funds Rate." *Federal Reserve Bank of St. Louis Review*, vol. 83, no. 4, 33–47.

Taylor, John B. (2007a). "Do We Get More Out of Theory Than We Put In?" *Central Banking*, vol. 18, no. 2, 23–27.

Taylor, John B. (2007b). "Globalization and Monetary Policy: Missions Impossible," poolside talk, Gerona, Spain, NBER conference, later published in Mark Gertler and Jordi Gali (Eds.), *The International Dimensions of Monetary Policy*. Chicago: The University of Chicago Press, 2009, pp. 609–624.

Taylor, John B. (2007c). "Housing and Monetary Policy," Federal Reserve Bank of Kansas City, *Proceedings–Economic Policy Symposium–Jackson Hole*, pp. 463–476.

Taylor, John B. (2008). "The Costs and Benefits of Deviating from the Systematic Component of Monetary Policy." Keynote Address at the Federal Reserve Bank of San Francisco, Conference on Monetary Policy and Asset Markets, February 22; https://web.stanford.edu/~johntayl/Onlinepapers combinedbyyear/2008/The_Costs_and_Benefits_of_Deviating_from_the _Systematic_Component_of_Monetary_Policy.pdf.

Taylor, John B. (2010). "The Fed and the Crisis: A Reply to Ben Bernanke." *Wall Street Journal*, January 11, p. A19.

Taylor, John B. (2011). "Legislating a Rule for Monetary Policy." *Cato Journal*, vol. 31, no. 3, 407–415.

Taylor, John B. (2012a). "The Dual Nature of Forecast Targeting and Instrument Rules," in *The Taylor Rule and the Transformation of Monetary Policy*, Evan F. Koenig, Robert Leeson, and George A. Kahn, eds. Stanford, CA: Hoover Institution Press, pp. 235–244.

Taylor, John B. (2012b). "Monetary Policy Rules Work and Discretion Doesn't: A Tale of Two Eras." *Journal of Money, Credit and Banking*, vol. 44, no. 6, 1017–1032.

Taylor, John B. (2013). "International Monetary Coordination and the Great Deviation," *Journal of Policy Modeling*, vol. 35, no. 3, 463–472.

Taylor, John. (2015). "Recreating the 1940s-Founded Institutions for Today's Global Economy." Remarks upon Receiving the Truman Medal for Economic Policy, Kansas City, MO, October 14. https://web.stanford.edu/~johntayl /2015_pdfs/Truman_Medal_Talk-Taylor-10-14-2015.pdf.

Taylor, John B. (2016a). "Independence and the Scope of the Central Bank's Mandate," *Sveriges Riksbank Economic Review*, no. 3.

Taylor, John B. (2016b). "A Rules-Based Cooperatively-Managed International Monetary System for the Future," in *International Monetary Cooperation: Lessons from the Plaza Accord After Thirty Years*, C.F. Bergsten and Russell Green, eds., Peterson Institute for International Economics: Washington, pp. 217–236.

Taylor, John B. (2016c). "The Staying Power of Staggered Wage and Price Setting Models in Macroeconomics." In *Handbook of Macroeconomics, Vol. 2*, John B. Taylor and Harald Uhlig, eds. Amsterdam: Elsevier Science, pp. 2009–2042.

Taylor, John B. (2018). "Alternatives for Reserve Balances and the Fed's Balance Sheet in the Future," in *The Structural Foundations of Monetary Policy*, Michael Bordo, John Cochrane, and Amit Seru, eds., Stanford, CA: Hoover Institution Press, pp. 16–27.

Taylor, John B., and Volker Wieland. (2012). "Surprising Comparative Properties of Monetary Models: Results from a New Model Data Base." *Review of Economics and Statistics*, vol. 94, no. 3, 800–816.

Taylor, John B., and Volker Wieland. (2016). "Finding the Equilibrium Real Interest Rate in a Fog of Policy Deviations." *Business Economics*, vol. 51, no. 3, 147–154.

Taylor, John B. and John C. Williams. (2009). "A Black Swan in the Money Market," *American Economic Journal: Macroeconomics*, vol. 1, no. 1, pp. 58–83

Taylor, John B., and John C. Williams. (2011). "Simple and Robust Rules for Monetary Policy," in *Handbook of Monetary Economics, Vol. 3*, Benjamin Friedman and Michael Woodford, eds. Amsterdam: Elsevier, pp. 829–859.

Teryoshin, Yevgeniy. (2017). "Historical Performance of Rule-Like Monetary Policy." Working Paper No. 17–005, Stanford Institute for Economic Policy Research, February; https://siepr.stanford.edu/sites/default/files/publications/17-005.pdf.

Thornton, Henry. (1939). *An Enquiry into the Nature and Effects of the Paper Credit of Great Britain.* Edited with an introduction by F. A. Hayek. New York: Rinehart & Company, Inc. Originally published in 1802.

Tinbergen, Jan. (1959). "An Economic Policy for 1936," in *Jan Tinbergen, Selected Papers*, L. H. Klaassen, L. M. Koyck, and H. J. Witteveen, eds. Amsterdam: North-Holland Publishing Company, pp. 37–84. Originally published in 1936 in Dutch.

Volcker, Paul. (2014). "Remarks," Bretton Woods Committee Annual Meeting, June 17, 2014; http://www.brettonwoods.org/sites/default/files/publications/Paul%20Volcker%20final%20Remarks%20June%2017.pdf.

Wicksell, Knut. (1907). "The Influence of the Rate of Interest on Prices." *Economic Journal*, vol. 17, 213–220.

Wieland, Volker, E. Afanasyeva, M. Kuete, and J. Yoo. (2016). "New Methods for Macro Financial Model Comparison and Policy Analysis," in *Handbook of Macroeconomics, Vol. 2*, John B Taylor and Harald Uhlig, eds. Amsterdam: Elsevier, pp. 1241-1319.

Williams, John C. (2003). "Simple Rules for Monetary Policy," *Federal Reserve Bank of San Francisco Economic Review*, pp. 1-12.

Williams, Rob. (2018). "Kudlow: Jerome Powell's 'Rules-Based' Fed Policy Is Promising," *Newsmax*, February 27; https://www.newsmax.com/finance/streettalk/larry-kudlow-jerome-powell-taylor-rule-inflation/2018/02/27/id/845817/.

Woodford, Michael. (2012). "Forecast Targeting as a Monetary Policy Strategy: Policy Rules in Practice," in *The Taylor Rule and the Transformation of Monetary Policy*, Evan F. Koenig, Robert Leeson and George A. Kahn, eds. Stanford, CA: Hoover Institution Press, pp. 185–233.

Yellen, Janet. (2012). "The Economic Outlook and Monetary Policy, *Money Marketeers*, New York, April 11. https://www.federalreserve.gov/newsevents/speech/files/yellen20120411a.pdf.

Yellen, Janet. (2015). "Monetary Policy and the State of the Economy." Testimony Before the Financial Services Committee, House of Representatives, February 25.

Yellen, Janet L. (2017a). "The Economic Outlook and the Conduct of Monetary Policy." Speech at the Stanford Institute for Economic Policy Research, Stanford University, January 19.

Yellen, Janet L. (2017a). "The Goals of Monetary Policy and How We Pursue Them." Speech at the Commonwealth Club, San Francisco, January 18.

Yun, Tack. (1996). "Nominal Price Rigidity, Money Supply Endogeneity, and Business Cycles," *Journal of Monetary Economics*, vol. 37, 345–370.

# Index